Westminster
Palace and Parliament

Westminster

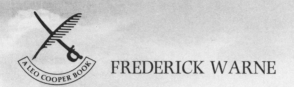

FREDERICK WARNE

PALACE & PARLIAMENT

by Patrick Cormack

with an Introduction by
THE RT HON GEORGE THOMAS MP
Speaker of the House of Commons

Title-page: *Westminster* c. *1770, by Antonio Joli—by courtesy of Leggatt Brothers.*

To Mary

ISBN 7232 2681 4

First published 1981 by
FREDERICK WARNE LTD
40 Bedford Square
London WC1B 3HE

Designed by John Mitchell
Printed in Great Britain by
BAS Printers Limited,
Over Wallop, Hampshire

Contents

Illustrations

ACKNOWLEDGEMENTS TO THE ILLUSTRATIONS

Unless separately acknowledged in the list of illustrations the originals of all the subjects belong to the Palace of Westminster. Special thanks are due to the Speaker and Works of Art Committee for permission to reproduce them and to the Serjeant at Arms and his staff for all the help they afforded both John Mitchell and me.

Introduction

by THE RT HON GEORGE THOMAS MP
Speaker of the House of Commons

When Edmund Burke, Member of Parliament for Bristol, proclaimed, 'England is the Mother of Parliaments', he was not to know that he had coined a phrase which would endure, and which would be universally applied to the Palace of Westminster itself. No other Parliament building in the world is better known or admired than Barry's majestic structure at Westminster. The beautiful pinnacles of the Victoria Tower and the dominating round face of Big Ben have become London's symbols right across the world.

To serve as a Member of Parliament in Westminster is a privilege beyond measure. Only the oddest of persons given that trust fails to develop a deep affection not only for the institution of Parliament, but for the building itself.

Even when Parliament is in recess it is impossible to walk through the corridors of the Palace or through either of its Chambers without a deep sense of awe. It enjoys an impressive atmosphere which, though intangible, is very real. The genius of Barry and Pugin's co-operative endeavours provided the country with one of the world's architectural miracles. Its exterior majesty is matched by an interior dignity that cannot easily be described in words.

Our Parliamentary Democracy is not an act of God; it is the heritage we enjoy as a result of the activities of men and women who through past centuries have fought for liberty, for freedom of speech, and for equality before the law. The only guarantee that we shall always have a freely elected Parliament answerable to the people, is constant vigilence by us all.

The alternative to our own present Parliamentary system is two fold, and neither picture is attractive. A one party state inexorably ensures its own permanent hold on power, even though it goes through the motions of an election. On the other hand, a dictatorship can never afford the luxury of freedom of speech, or equality before the law. The only system that protects the rights of all is Parliamentary Democracy. As Winston Churchill reminded us, although it is a cumbersome and often inefficient system, it is the best available to us.

One of the essential steps for the protection of Parliament is to ensure that our citizens know the remarkable story of how our system has evolved. To know our history is to be proud to be British.

In this book Patrick Cormack gives life and significance to the saga of Westminster. His dedicated and detailed research adds enormously to our store of knowledge. As the book moves through the story of our yesterdays, it is as gripping as a thriller. It could have been written only by one who has a deep love and loyalty for the institution of Parliament.

The periodical pettiness of our predecessors in Parliament makes painful reading, but none the less has a moral for M.P.'s in every generation.

This book is a masterpiece which should become a standard work for everyone interested in Parliament. It should certainly be part of every school and college library.

In my judgement this study of *Westminster : Palace and Parliament,* is a work of art worthy of its subject. There can be no higher praise.

GEORGE THOMAS

Preface

Soon after I entered the House of Commons in 1970 I began conducting parties of constituents and others around the Palace of Westminster. The questions I was asked, and often could not answer, helped me to increase my own knowledge of a building I had always reckoned as one of the finest in Europe. But in my search for answers I rapidly discovered that there was no readily available up-to-date book on the Palace for the general reader. There were short guides (of which the official guide is by far the best), excellent picture books and fascinating works on procedure, but no work that sought to tell the history and geography of the building in reasonable detail.

The book is an attempt to fill that gap. It does not seek to rival either the scholars' text books on Parliamentary practice or the detailed study of the art and architecture brought out by H. M. Port and his colleagues in 1976. However, I hope it will serve a useful purpose and help to enlighten all those who are fascinated by this greatest of all 'people's palaces', at once the home of Western democracy and the greatest building of the last century.

To all those who have helped me with my enquiries and encouraged me in my efforts I am most grateful, particularly to Mr Speaker who has contributed the Foreword; to the Librarian and staff of the House of Commons Library for their unfailingly courteous and efficient help; to Mr Philip Wright who helped me select the illustrations; to Jock Black and Ian Stanley who assisted me with the research and to Jane Willoughby and her sister who typed the manuscript. To Tom Hartman, my editor and John Mitchell, who designed the book and took the photographs, I am especially grateful but my final and warmest thanks must go to my wife who typed the first manuscript and who has been unfailingly encouraging—and tolerant.

Westminster, 1980   PATRICK CORMACK

The Dreadful Calamity

THE regular congregation of St Margaret's, Westminster arrived on Sunday 19 October, 1834 to find the doors locked and a notice proclaiming that 'In consequence of the dreadful calamity that has befallen the Lords and Commons, a great portion of the books, records, etc., having been placed in this Church for safety, Divine Service cannot be performed . . .'

There were many sightseers in Westminster that morning who had come to see what Saturday's *Morning Herald* had described as 'the black ruins of those proud halls where the Parliament of England has — through good report and bad — through glory or shame — so long held its meetings.' For the 'dreadful calamity' was the fire which had engulfed the vast and rambling Palace of Westminster just three days previously, reducing almost all but the great Westminster Hall itself, and the rather insignificant Jewel Tower on the other side of Old Palace Yard, to a labyrinth of scarred masonry and piles of charred rubble. It had been a spectacular fire and descriptions of its raging, and speculations about its origin, had occupied most of the columns of the London Press since.

Even those who most regretted the general devastation (and many did not) waxed eloquent on the fantastic pyrotechnic display. It had presented 'a spectacle, as viewed from Lambeth, and in as lovely a moonlight night as could be conceived, horridly beautiful'. Turner and Constable both captured something of the majesty of the conflagration, and a host of less distinguished artists felt inspired to take advantage of public interest by peddling quickly drawn sketches — the more vivid the better — to illustrate the numerous and graphic 'descriptions' that poured from the presses. The coincidence of spectacle — and there had been no fire to compare with this since the Great Fire of 1666 — and subject were too good an opportunity to miss.

The fire marked the end of a landmark and of an era. It was eight hundred years since a King had first held his Court at Westminster and the Palace had been the birthplace of Parliament. It had ceased to be a royal residence in the sixteenth century and though it was still a royal Palace it was as 'Parliament' that it was known. The Chambers, dining rooms, libraries and numerous apartments that had been adapted or added over the centuries housed Lords and Commons in circumstances varying from uncomfortable splendour to dangerous squalor.

The fire had begun in the House of Lords with an attempt to dispose of the notched tally sticks, which had, until eight years previously,

The Painted Chamber after the fire, 1834. One of a series of water colours by Thomas Clark.

1

been used as receipts for sums paid to the Exchequer. From the time of William I official accounts had been kept in this way. Short rods of hazel or willow were notched to indicate the sums paid and then split, one piece being given to the debtor as a receipt, and the other preserved by the Exchequer as a record.

Dickens, who, as a young reporter, witnessed the fire, years later entertained the audience at Drury Lane with a droll account of the whole procedure: 'Ages ago a savage mode of keeping accounts on notched sticks was introduced into the Court of Exchequer and the accounts were kept much as Robinson Crusoe kept his calendar on the desert island . . . Official routine inclined to these notched sticks, as if they were pillars of the constitution . . . In the reign of George III an enquiry was made by some revolutionary spirit whether—pens, ink and paper, slates and pencils, being in existence—this obstinate adherence to an obsolete custom ought to be continued and whether a change ought not to be effected. All the red tape of the country grew redder at this bold and original conception and it took until 1826 to get the sticks abolished. In 1834 it was found that there was a considerable accumulation of them; and the question then arose— what was to be done with such worn out, worm-eaten rotten old bits

Two views of the Great Fire. Left a contemporary print, one of those produced in vast numbers showing the Lords and the Commons aflame, from Old Palace Yard. Right a little-known view of the fire from the river by David Hall McKewan.

of wood? The sticks were housed at Westminster and it would naturally occur to any intelligent person that nothing could be easier than to allow them to be carried away as firewood by the miserable people who lived in the neighbourhood. However, they never had been useful and official routine required that they never should be, and so the order went through that they should privately and confidentially burn. It came to pass that they were burnt in a stove in the House of Lords. The stove, over-gorged with these preposterous sticks, set fire to the panelling; the panelling set fire to the House of Lords; the House of Lords set fire to the House of Commons; and two Houses were reduced to ashes . . .'

This is precisely what did happen. On the morning of 16 October two workmen began to get rid of several cartloads of the remaining tallies by burning them in a stove which heated the House of Lords. They obviously worked extremely hard. The Clerk of the Works, Richard Whibley, who had decided not to burn the tallies in the Exchequer Yard for fear of alarming the neighbourhood and provoking the police, looked in three times during the day to make sure that they were stoking and not stealing. During the afternoon Mrs Wright, a deputy Housekeeper in the House of Lords, was showing visitors over when they noticed smoke and remarked on the heat of the stone floor. Mrs Wright made enquiries of the workmen but they said that they were merely carrying out orders and that they would be finished shortly. At five o'clock they went home and Mrs Wright locked up.

An hour later a doorkeeper's wife was coming in and called out, 'Oh, good God, the House of Lords is on fire.' Mrs Wright was not especially alarmed. She thought it was the matting, and that had caused trouble before, but on investigating she found Black Rod's Box in flames and ran for help. She met Richard Whibley, who seemed 'perfectly petrified' at the news, and then dashed into the street to raise the alarm.

The flames spread rapidly and, though men of the newly established Metropolitan Police soon arrived, and fire engines were quickly on the scene, there was little that could be done to contain the blaze. It had taken too firm a hold and the Palace was too full of dry combustible material for the efforts, however prodigious, of early nineteenth century fire-fighters and their equipment to prevail. Not that their job was made any easier by the vast crowds which quickly swarmed in by road or river; by the strong wind from the south-west; or by the difficulty of getting a proper water supply.

The morning after the fire—a view from Old Palace Yard.

Detachments of the Grenadier Guards and the Coldstream Guards arrived to assist the police in maintaining an open space before the building to let the firemen get on as best they might. But their efforts were not helped by the number of illustrious fire-fighters—Lord Melbourne, the Prime Minister, among them—who dashed to the scene to render assistance. In the words of one eye witness, 'The firemen shouted their directions from above, to the numerous, busy, meddling people, whose rank embarrassed but whose wisdom afforded little guide from below.' In the words of the same observer, 'There was the greatest want of unity of design and sagacious vigour of proceedings. There was zealous interference on all sides but the great want of a Commander-in-Chief.'

Almost all reliable witnesses later agreed, however, that it was highly unlikely that the fire could have been arrested, or more salvaged from it, even had its fighting been better co-ordinated and controlled. By the time it was discovered it had taken too firm a hold.

By half past seven the House of Lords was virtually gutted and the Commons already alight. 'The scene at this time was grand and terrific. The flames shot up to a great height, and obscured the light of the moon, increasing, rather than diminishing, the apparent darkness of the night, and contrasting in a striking manner the brilliant light which they threw upon the surrounding objects with the general blackness of the sky. Not only the streets in the vicinity, but the different bridges were now covered with immense multitudes gazing with mingled awe and admiration on the scene of destruction.'

By nine o'clock the whole of the three Regiments of Guards were in attendance, and by ten they had been joined by the Royal

Horse Guards from the Regent's Park Barracks. They all struggled to help the fire-fighters rescue what could be salvaged from the blaze, and to try to prevent its spreading to Westminster Hall.

Soon after the fire was discovered Sir John Cam Hobhouse, Melbourne's Commissioner for Woods and Works, had arrived on the scene and taken charge of the operation. He had immediately given directions for the removal of public records, 'an operation which he actively and anxiously superintended'. All manner of vehicles— hackney coaches, cabs and waggons—were requisitioned to take the precious papers to places of safety. Many were taken to private houses nearby but most went to the various Government offices around Whitehall. By half past ten most of the furniture of the Exchequer and other law courts had been removed to the pavements opposite Poet's Corner, and by the time the fire reached the Speaker's House many of the portraits, and some of the other valuable property it contained, had been removed.

The losses, however, were great. The Rolls of Parliament, containing the signatures of generations of Members, were the most valuable of the documents that were destroyed; but they were not the only ones. Apart from the manuscript journals, the main collection of House of Commons papers was lost, as were most of the books from the recently established library. One sorry tale is told in a contemporary account: 'At eleven o'clock an express was received by Mr Cooper, Secretary to the Record Board, at his house in the country. He arrived at twelve o'clock and found that in the early part of the evening, nearly the whole of the extremely valuable records of the Augmentation Office, upon the repairing and arrangement of which so many thousand pounds had been spent in the last four years, had

5

been thrown out of the windows and removed in various ways, some to the King's Mews, but the greater part to St Margaret's Church. A vast number of the most ancient, in the course of this operation, unfortunately fell out of the bags and were scattered about the street. A number of soldiers, under the direction of Mr Cooper, were employed during the whole night, in collecting these; and large numbers were recovered saturated with water and very much defaced.'

One document of enormous constitutional importance was, however, discovered after the fire virtually unharmed—the death warrant of Charles I.

Fortunately the wind dropped and to this, coupled with the exertions of those who stripped neighbouring roofs, we owe the saving of Westminster Hall. By three o'clock in the morning of 17 October it was clear that the Hall was safe, but the official report of the damage compiled the following day indicated just what had been lost.

In the House of Lords the Chamber itself, the Robing Rooms, the Committee Rooms on the West Front, 'and the rooms of the resident officers as far as the Octagon Tower at the south end of the building,'

Three subjects from a set of watercolours by Thomas Clark painted after the Great Fire. Left *St Stephen's Chapel from the Speaker's Gallery.* Centre *the Long Gallery, House of Lords.* Right *exterior view of the Painted Chamber.*

together with the Painted Chamber, were all almost totally destroyed, as was the north end of the Royal Gallery. In the House of Commons the skeleton of the Chamber and four Committee Rooms and the State Dining Room were all that was capable of being repaired.

As for contents: 'The furniture, fixtures and fittings to both the Houses of Lords and Commons, with the Committee Rooms belonging thereto, is with few exceptions destroyed.' It was a dismal catalogue.

Remarkably no one was killed during the blaze although nine people were taken to Westminster Hospital with severe injuries and a great many of the fire-fighters received minor ones.

It was these accidents, 'the sense that the property of respectable persons was in course of destruction and that lives of many brave and honest men were in jeopardy, which alone controlled a universal disposition to merriment', according to one observer of the multitude—'in the crowded boats that floated on the river—or the countless number that swarmed upon the bridges, the wharfs, and even upon the housetops.'

Eye witness accounts abound in reports of the pleasantries that were exchanged as each new section was engulfed in flames. Just before Parliament had been prorogued, a Select Committee of the Commons, chaired by a radical Member, Joseph Hume, had recommended the vacating of the present premises and the building of new. Now the word went round that, 'Joe Hume's Motion is being passed without a division'. One correspondent recalls, 'Instead of regretting the event as a natural calamity, many appear to consider it as a merited visitation and actually openly expressed their regrets that the Lords and Commons were not sitting at the time.' These sentiments were echoed in a quaintly ponderous document issued within forty-eight hours and beginning, 'Oh fire, Outrageous innovator! Thou art, indeed, no Tory, nor yet a Whig. Yea, verily thou hast outradicalled the hottest radical—out-Cromwelled Cromwell, and realised the dreams of old Guy Faux'.

Those who currently express concern that Parliament and politicians have fallen into disrepute could do worse than thumb through the yellowing pages of the papers that record the Great Fire, or glance at some of the splendidly irreverent cartoons of the period. The thought of 'great' and generally pompous people being discomforted has been the very stuff of popular humour for centuries. The fire provided ample material for it. But though the mob cheered each collapse of masonry they 'were favourable to the Hall, the fine old Hall. Love of that is universal.'

No one was less upset about the destruction of Parliament than one of its newest Members, William Cobbett. He was in Ireland at the time but he made no attempt to hide his feelings of exultation when he wrote in his *Register* on 20 October, 'Here am I having last evening been received with acclamation of joy by thirty thousand men . . . when in comes the London post this morning bringing in my incipid old friend and neighbour the *Morning Herald* an account of the burning of the Parliament House. Whether the cause be fire and brimstone from heaven or by the less sublime agency, "Swing", my friend the *Herald* does not tell me . . . But my friend . . . says that the mob (meaning the people of London) "when they saw the progress of the flames raised a savage shout of exultation". Did they indeed? The *Herald* exclaims "Oh unreflecting people!" Now perhaps "the mob" exulted because "the mob" was really a reflecting "mob". When even a horse or dog receives any treatment that it does not like it always shuns the place where it got the treatment . . . There is always a connection in our minds between sufferings we undergo and the place in which they were inflicted, or the place in which they originate.'

Cobbett then gives a long list of the Measures enacted in Parliament by which 'the mob' had through the centuries suffered, continuing, 'With regard to what is to be done in consequence of this fire; how the fire came to take place; what Mother Jordan's offspring thought of the ruins and ashes when they inspected them (a reference to the visit of William IV's illegitimate sons) as the base reporters tell us they did . . . these . . . are matter to be more fully dealt with . . . But I must say that those who talk of this matter as a mere fire do not, may it please their

Specimens of Stained Glass from St Stephens Chapel.

Fragments of stained glass from St Stephen's Chapel.

reportership, reflect. It is a great event; come from what cause it might, it is a great event.'

The fact that Cobbett's sentiments had been so vociferously anticipated whilst the fire raged, inevitably gave rise to speculation as to its cause. There were those who immediately associated it with 'Captain Swing'—the name by which those who went in for rural incendiarism at the time were generally known, and when it emerged that one of the labourers employed on burning the tallies had been in jail, and that the other was an Irish Roman Catholic, suspicion was further aroused. The *Morning Post* carried an account, 'that on Thursday last a person who was travelling by coach from Hereford to London arrived at Cheltenham about half past eight o'clock where he was told "A dreadful fire has broken out in London and burnt down the House of Lords". Cheltenham is nearly one hundred miles from London and this account had reached that place within two hours of the commencement of the fire.'

Then there was the widely circulated story of James Cooper, an ironfounder, who alleged that he had been in the Bush Inn, Dudley, one hundred and twenty-seven miles from London on the night, when, soon after ten o'clock, he had heard that the House of Lords was burned to the ground. This one was taken seriously enough to be thoroughly investigated by a Committee of the Privy Council but when they looked into it they concluded that Cooper's story was full of contradictions and 'wholly unsupported'. It would be difficult, they reported 'to point out a fire which could be more clearly traced than this has been to its cause, without suspicion of evil design'.

Stories proliferated, too, of looting and of drunkenness and even of cowardice by those fighting the fire. They were suitably disposed of by Joseph Hume in a letter to *The Times* which he concluded as follows: 'In the zeal, order and number of the military and police, and the daring of the firemen, nothing was wanting; in the power of the engines, the quantity of water and the general superintendence of the whole operations a lamentable deficiency was apparent.'

Speculation about the fire's cause, and about the conduct of those who fought it soon subsided, but the controversy over what should happen next continued. For years there had been discontent about the accommodation of Parliament, culminating in Joseph Hume's Committee Report. Now something had to be done. The question was, what? Should there be an attempt to restore such of the buildings that were capable of repair: to patch and to add? Should everything that was left be razed to the ground and a new Parliament House built at Westminster? Or should Parliament meet elsewhere? Powerful arguments were advanced in favour of each proposition, though the one that received least support was the last.

As early as the day after the fire the debate was joined with a leading article in *The Times* which concluded, 'The old Houses of Parliament with all their inconveniences, with all the absurd disproportion, at least in the lower House, in accommodation to numbers, might have from session to session, echoed the complaints of their imprisoned Members, and but for the blind and terrible agency might have occupied for years to come the collective wisdom of three nations.'

The occasion of these remarks was an offer by William IV of his new Palace in The Mall, Buckingham Palace, as a place for Parliament to meet. It was an offer that was obviously seriously meant and certainly the Palace would have provided an adequate meeting place, at least on a temporary basis. However, the ties of Westminster were strong and there were those who feared that once this offer or any similar one were accepted (St James's Palace was also suggested) Lords and Commons would never return 'home'.

Though it was decided, therefore, that there must be some patching and repairing to enable Parliament's business to be carried on in the ruins, it was soon resolved that this should only be a temporary expedient, until a new and fitting Parliament House was built at Westminster.

Many of those frustrated worshippers would have been reminded by the *Sunday Times* when they returned from St Margaret's that morning that, 'Foreigners stared with unaffected astonishment at learning it was in that dreary and confined apartment that the millions were voted that secured foreign potentates in their palaces.' The writer acknowledges that 'demands on the national purse, and the public impatience' had been so great, 'that the building of a new House was deferred from time to time . . .' and of course, 'many of the Members were reluctant to destroy that edifice where so many great men had acted a conspicuous part . . .' But it had now been destroyed and the question, as far as most serious politicians and reporters were concerned, was not *if* the Palace should be replaced, or if it should be at Westminster, but when, and in what form the new one should be built. There were many views on that but on one thing there was near general agreement. The new Palace must incorporate the great Hall of the old, 'this most venerable relic of the olden time, the ruin of which, with all its historical associations, could not be compensated for by as many modern trumpery structures that would suffice to cover a wilderness.'

CHAPTER ONE

Westminster Hall

Oh! 'Damn the House of Commons, let it blaze,
But save, Oh! Save the Hall!
Were words which must devotion raise,
Within the breasts of great and small.

THE fire that engulfed and destroyed the Palace, to the delight of so many who watched the blaze, answered their even more fervent prayer: it spared the Hall. The prayer has been repeated and answered twice since.

Over one hundred years later at the height of the blitz (10/11 May, 1941) the Hall was again spared, though the Commons Chamber was ravaged by fire and completely destroyed. Thirty-three years after that, on 17 June, 1974, it survived an I.R.A. bomb.

And so this greatest of medieval halls, with the Tower of London one of the two most historic secular buildings in the land, still stands substantially unaltered after six hundred years of political change and turmoil, the proud symbol of the continuing link of Crown and Parliament, and a national shrine such as no other part of the Palace of Westminster, indeed no other royal Palace, can possibly be.

Although, with its mighty hammer beam roof and the statues of early kings looking down, it is still the scene of great formal pomp and ceremony, as when Queen Elizabeth II was presented with the Loyal Addresses of Parliament at the beginning of her Silver Jubilee celebrations, it is also the only room in any of our royal Palaces which is open throughout the year to all who care to come and look.

The Hall we see now is Richard II's but though he added and he altered he did not establish. Westminster Hall dates from the end of the eleventh century when William Rufus, son of the Conqueror, determined to erect a great and magnificent hall as the centre of a palace which would be the wonder of Europe.

It took two years to build and was an immense size for the times: two hundred and thirty-nine feet six inches long, and sixty-seven feet six inches wide, with walls rising to a height of nearly twenty feet to a gallery running round the four sides of the Hall. There was thus an arcade of small rounded Norman arches forming a continuous pattern with the windows, reminiscent of the clerestory in the transept of Winchester Cathedral.

Impressive as the Hall was, it did not impress the king. Returning from Normandy to celebrate his Whitsuntide Feast at Westminster in

A 13th century statue of Edward I—one of a group in Westminster Hall.

1099 he expressed great disappointment, according to Matthew Paris, the thirteenth-century historian. He thought it not nearly large enough: 'It is a mere bed-chamber compared with what I intended to build.'

Bed-chamber or not, he had little time to enjoy or to curse it. Within a year he was dead, slain by an arrow whilst out hunting in the New Forest. He was one of the least appealing of our early kings but the hall he created was a great enough bequest to earn the pardon of posterity, if not a smooth passage through purgatory. His brother, Henry I, who succeeded him, made Westminster his principal seat and summoned his first great Council there, 'all chief men of England, both laity and clergy', at Michaelmas in 1102. The Council would probably have met in the Great Hall. Certainly it was here that he agreed what we regard as the most abiding achievement of his reign, the foundation of the judicial system—to the firm establishment of which the great reforms of his grandson, Henry II, contributed so much.

During his reign the Hall became, in effect, the centre of the nation's administrative life, the seat of royal power, of government, and of justice. Here the King kept Whitsun and Christmas and the other great festivals. Here betrothals and marriages were celebrated. Here the King feasted, dispensed lavish hospitality and held audience. Successive kings spent considerable sums on adorning the Hall: Henry II, Richard I (who spent only six months of his reign in the Kingdom), Henry III, Edward I—all had a hand in its restoration, extension or embellishment.

Throughout the early years the Hall was the scene of many dramatic events, as when Henry III's Council of 'Archbishops, Bishops, Abbots, Priors, Knights, Templars and Hospitallers, Earls, Barons, Rectors of Churches and Tenants in Chief' met at Westminster on the second Sunday after Easter, 1229, to resist the demands of the Pope for a tithe (a tenth) of all the moveables in England and Ireland, a demand which had already been secretly conceded by the King. The Council, however, was not so easily coerced and it was only the threat of ex-communication which finally persuaded them to grant the Papal demands, though even then, Ranulph, Earl of Chester, refused.

Henry's was a turbulent reign. His love of art and beauty, as expressed in his great rebuilding of Westminster Abbey and in the expansion and enrichment of the Palace of Westminster (the decoration of the Painted Chamber was at his command), was not matched by his statecraft. He squandered the royal revenue on his Queen's friends and kinsmen and came into frequent conflict with his Councils as a result. In 1252 he summoned Londoners to the Hall. He announced that he was going on the crusade and implored them to give him money to finance the expedition. They knew their King. Only three citizens came forward. The King summoned another Council and, desperate for revenue, pledged that he would submit to ex-communication if he did not keep his word this time.

New Palace Yard before the fire.

There followed one of the most extraordinary scenes ever witnessed in the Hall. Holding the King to his word the Council assembled on 3 May, 1252. Each man, save the King, held a lighted taper in his hand—he refused to hold a candle because he was not a Priest, but to show his integrity he kept his hand on his breast. Whilst he stood there the words of anathema were pronounced by Boniface, Archbishop of Canterbury, who called down the curse of God upon any who should, in future, violate the two great charters—Magna Carta and the Charter of Forests. Henry again swore to observe and confirm them. Every man then cast his taper upon the floor of the Hall whilst the Archbishop prayed that the souls of all who should break the Charters, 'might thus be extinguished and stink and smoke in Hell'. The King himself added: 'So may God help me. I will inviolably observe all these things, as I am a man and a Christian, a Knight and an anointed King.' By the turn of the year, following an appeal to Rome in which he alleged that he had acted under stress, he had obtained absolution from his oath and was back to his former tricks.

Such duplicity could not go unchallenged, and it was in response to it that a towering figure, one of the greatest ever to be associated with Parliament, emerged—Simon de Montfort. It was he who led the Barons' Rebellion against the fickle King and who captured him at the Battle of Lewes in 1264. A year later de Montfort's famous Parliament met, in the Chapter House of the Abbey. This was the first time the cities and the boroughs, as well as the shires, sent representatives to the Great Council, the first time the Commons were summoned to debate with the Prelates and magnates of the realm.

A precedent had been truly established and during the reign of Edward I (the Hammer of the Scots), who was determined to be as different from his father as possible, Westminster Hall came into its own. It was here that Edward ('the father of the mother of Parliaments') held his first Parliament, on 19 May, 1275, a Parliament which included citizens and burgesses and 'is memorable as the first lawfully convened and a genuinely representative Parliament . . . Not only was the Commons present but they were specifically stated to have given their consent to the Statute of Westminster, and to another Statute which granted the King the customs on wool and leather, thereby for the first time giving legal foundation to this form of revenue.' With the money given him the King raised an army to subdue Llewellyn, Prince of Wales, who had refused to do him homage. Deserted by his friends, Llewellyn was forced to submit, but he was treated with great chivalry by Edward and spent Christmas with him at Westminster in 1277.

It was during Edward's reign that the division of the King's Court into the Court of Exchequer, concerned with revenue, the Court of Common Pleas, called to hear suits between private persons, and the King's Bench, which tried all matters connected with the Sovereign or reserved for judgement, was finally worked out. To these three Courts, each with its own set of judges, a fourth was added, the Court of

Chancery, the Lord Chancellor's special Court where all those petitions which 'besought the King either to mitigate the harshness of the common law or to supply its deficiencies' were examined. Although the courts did not always sit in Westminster Hall during Edward's reign it was certainly regarded as their natural home, indeed the exact location in the Hall of Exchequer, Common Pleas and King's Bench had been defined during the troubled reign of his father.

Sometimes the gaily decorated Hall — Edward had it freshly painted in 1278 — was used for special trials. One Thomas Turbeville was tried for 'adhering to the King's enemies' (treason) in 1259, and was sentenced to death. However, the first major trial to be held here was the trial by special commission in August, 1305, of William Wallace, who, after briefly commanding much of Scotland and the north of England had been defeated by Edward at Falkirk and captured near Glasgow. He was brought to London in chains and his arrival at the Hall was made a public spectacle.

Edward was determined to make an example of him. He was charged with treason, with burning towns and monasteries and with murdering the King's subjects. His defence was simple. 'I cannot be a traitor to Edward for I owe him no allegiance. He is not my God; he never received my homage and whilst life is in this persecuted body he shall never receive it . . . As Governor of my country I have been enemy to its enemies. I have slain the English. I have mortally opposed the English King.' Because he had despoiled church property and killed clerks he would repent but 'It is not of Edward of England that I shall ask pardon'. The sentence was a foregone conclusion. Wallace was the first great figure to be found guilty of treason in the Hall and to suffer the foul indignities of a traitor's death — dragged to the gibbet, hanged, drawn, his heart burned before his face, and his body quartered.

But it was not the trial of Wallace that was the most important event to take place in the Hall during Edward's reign. That distinction belongs to the great Model Parliament of 1295. The Archbishops, Bishops, the greater Abbots, seven Earls and forty-one Barons were all summoned by name, as were representatives of the lower ranks of the clergy and of the laity who had elected from among their number, and on the order of the royal sheriffs, two knights from each shire, two citizens from each city and two burgesses from each Borough. Perhaps the most significant thing about the Parliament was the writ by which it was summoned and in which Edward stated, '*Quod omnes tangit ab omnibus approbretur*': what touches all should be approved by all. Democracy was not yet on the horizon but this certainly set the pattern for a truly representative Parliament. Though the Commons had been summoned before, it was only after the Model Parliament that their inclusion became the norm.

During the unhappy reign of Edward II (1307–1327), who was deposed and later murdered at Berkeley Castle, the law courts continued to sit in Westminster Hall and certain practices were

A 17th-century artist's impression of Henry III's confrontation with his Council on 3 May, 1252. The artist seems unaware that the hall he was familiar with did not emerge until after Richard II's reconstruction.

becoming well established customs. The Lord Chancellor, for instance, now invariably sat on a great bench of marble behind a marble table on a dais at the south end of the Hall—a table and bench which were used by the King when he presided over his Council or dined in state.

By Edward III's long reign (1327–1377) Parliament, though it met at Westminster, probably used other rooms for its meetings, but the

Hall was the setting for many great occasions. Here Edward made his son, later called the Black Prince, a Duke. Here was held the banquet to celebrate the victory of Poitiers when the French King John was received with all the chivalry befitting a royal guest by his royal captor. John was still an 'enforced house guest' at Christmas, 1358, when Edward held his feast in the Hall with another captured King by his side, David of Scotland.

It was another (and a lesser) King, Edward's grandson, Richard II (1377–1399) whose name will forever be most prominently associated with Westminster Hall. For it was in his reign that the Hall was altered beyond recognition and became the great and splendid building we know today.

The Hall needed repairing, but for Richard repair was not enough. He wished to get rid of the great row of wooden pillars that supported the roof and which caused difficulties when tables were spread or benches brought in for Lords and Commons. Like many of our weaker Kings, Richard was a man of culture, taste and artistic discernment, and he was singularly fortunate in having at his call Henry Yevele, the greatest of medieval master masons, and the supreme exponent of Gothic architecture, and Hugh Herland, finest of master carpenters. Between them they transformed the Hall from a Norman to a Gothic masterpiece.

The walls they kept, though they were much restored, but the gallery went and the Norman windows were replaced by perpendicular. At the north end they built a porch with a tower at either side and a great window, while at the southern end was another window with niches at each side containing the statues of Kings. But the chief glory was the roof. The columns went and new and mighty beams spanned the great expanse in one magnificent arch. The wood was oak from the King's park at Odiham in Hampshire, from the Abbot of St Albans' wood at Bernam and from Stoke Park, whence two hundred oaks were brought.

Many of the accounts still survive. They tell us, for instance, that £5.19s were paid to Edward Seymour, John Priour and Peter Scoriere, 'for the carriage of two hundred and four loads of oak timber lately brought from William Croyser in Stoke Park, thence to Ditton-on-Thames', and that 'to eight carters with their carts carrying twenty-six corbels from the same place to the aforesaid Ham, twenty-six journies', £6.10s was paid. It was a mammoth enterprise and the magnitude of it all helps to give us an appreciation of the achievements of the great medieval builders. So stout were the oaks used that in 1922, 'after more than five centuries of slow decay and the attacks of the deathwatch beetle, the largest baulks were found to be still more than two feet thick and the hollow gnawed in them by those noxious insects to be large enough to hold the body of a full grown man'. A great deal of the work was done at a place called 'The Frame' near Farnham in Surrey to which one hundred and fifty loads of timber were sent in June, 1395 alone. When they had been shaped the beams were taken apart and carted by road or brought by river to Westminster.

The roof, the most advanced and sophisticated of its age, and Herland's supreme achievement, was a hammer-beam roof. To obviate the necessity for pillars weight and thrust had to be distributed as low down as possible on Yevele's supporting walls, which had themselves been reinforced by massive buttresses. There could be no tie beam at the foot of the rafters for there was no timber that could span sixty-seven and a half feet—and so he joined the rafters half way along their length by means of a collar. 'The lower half of each pair of principals was then held rigid by strutts and braces in such a way as to reduce the thrust on the wall to a minimum. The hammer beam itself on which the main strutts supporting the principal rested projected from the top of the wall and was held up in its turn by a curved brace springing from the corbels built into the wall half way down them immediately below the window.' The strutts, braces, hammer beams and principals were tenonned together, thus ensuring the necessary rigidity.

As work progressed other artists were called in. One Robert Grassington carved the great angels on the hammer beams. Walter Walton placed his six statues of Kings on the niches in the south wall, three on either side of the great window.

Thus was created the Westminster Hall we know. However, before the work was finally completed Yevele was dead and Richard deposed—in Westminster Hall. Ever unstable, he had sought to rule as an absolute monarch but he had neither the presence nor the power to overawe. He temporarily established his supremacy and banished his cousin, Henry Bolingbroke, whom he had recently made Duke of Hereford, but when he went to Ireland, wrongly sensing it was safe to go, Bolingbroke returned at the head of a powerful force. Richard's supporters drifted away and when the first Parliament to meet in the new Great Hall assembled the King's chair was empty, for he was in the Tower. The proceedings were opened by the Archbishop of York who read Richard's forced renunciation. It was accepted and the sentence of deposition pronounced. Henry of Lancaster made his claim and it was acclaimed by Parliament. Parliament had helped to make a King.

By 1400 Westminster Hall was associated not only with the dispensing of justice and the meeting of Parliament. It was a centre of London trading, stall holders setting up their booths on either side of the Hall. Lydgate, the poet and contemporary of Chaucer, went to seek justice there and tells how he was accosted on either side:

> Where Fleming on me began for to cry,
> Master what will you copen or buy,
> Fine felt hat or spectacles to reade,
> Laye down yo' sylver, and hear you may speede.

Two and a half centuries later trade was still flourishing. Samuel

Three men who were sent to their deaths from Westminster Hall: Sir Thomas More, Bishop Fisher, the Earl of Essex.

Pepys refers to 'book buying expeditions' at Westminster Hall and Wycherley in *The Plain Dealer* writes:

> In the Hall of Westminster,
> Sleek seamstress vends amidst the Court her wares.

In the early eighteenth century it was a veritable bazaar. A visitor entering the Hall was 'surprised to see in the same place, men on the one side with baubles and toys, and the other taken up with the fear of judgement, on which depends their inevitable destiny. In this shop are sold ribbons and gloves, towels and commodes by word of mouth; in another shop lands and tenements are disposed of by decree. On your left hand you hear a nimble-tongued painted seamstress, with her charming treble invite you to buy some of her nicknacks; and on your right a deep-mouthed cryer demanding impossibilities: that silence be kept among women and lawyers.' During the same period we read of hireling witnesses parading themselves in the Hall, a straw behind the ear being the mark of identification. By the end of the eighteenth century commercial activity had almost ceased (although some stalls remained as late as 1880 when the Law Courts were removed to The Strand) but the Hall was often used for political meetings. There is a

spirited account of one held in February, 1780 in connection with a Westminster election petition attended by three thousand people and addressed by Wilkes, Fox and Burke. Handbills were distributed to excite the people against the Duke of Richmond, alleging he had been enriched by the Coal Tax.

But it is as a setting for state trials, and as the scene of Coronation Banquets, that the Hall is particularly associated from the fifteenth century onwards. In the sixteenth century, when trials were all too frequent, the most notable was that of Sir Thomas More. A brass plaque let into the floor today reminds visitors that this is where one of the greatest of all Englishmen was sentenced to death after a mockery of a trial in 1535.

It was ironical that he should have been 'tried' here, for, as Lord Chancellor after Wolsey, More had presided over the Court of Chancery in the Hall. 'The law's delay' was even then notorious and people were amazed by the expedition, as well as the equity, with which he dispensed true justice. It was his incorruptibility which led to More falling foul of his King. He was not prepared to recognise the validity of Henry's divorce, nor later his assumption of the title of Supreme Head of the Church of England.

Shortly before More's trial the saintly Bishop of Rochester, John Fisher, had been found guilty of the same 'treason' and beheaded. As with Fisher the verdict in More's case was never in doubt: 'Pity, mercy, equity nor justice had there no place'.

And yet it was More's finest hour. At the moment of his condemnation, worn out after months of imprisonment in the Tower, his faded clothing contrasting with the garish glitter all around, he made the noblest speech ever made in the Hall. He had shown how the charge rested on the perjury of Richard Rich. Now he challenged his indictment as, 'grounded upon an act of Parliament directly repugnant to the laws of God and his Holy Church.' As he saw it, 'This Kingdom alone, being but one member and a small part of the Church cannot make a particular law disagreeing with the general law of Christ's universal Catholic Church, no more than the City of London might enact a law against an Act of Parliament to be binding upon the whole realm.' He quoted Magna Carta, which promised immunity to the Church, and the King's Coronation Oath, when he was interrupted and reminded of all the 'Bishops, universities and most learned men in the Kingdom' who had subscribed to the Act. Why should he so vehemently argue against it? His reply was devastating. 'I am not bounden, my Lord, to conform my conscience to the Council of one realm against the Council of Christendom. For the aforesaid Holy Bishops, I have, for every Bishop of yours above, one hundred; and for one Council or Parliament of yours (God knows what manner of one) I have all the Councils made these thousand years. And for this one Kingdom I have all other Christian realms.' At the last neither his clarity nor his wit deserted him: 'I verily trust, and shall therefore right heartily pray, though your Lordships have now here in earth

CONCILIVM SEPTEM NOBILIVM ANGLORVM CONIVRANTIVM IN NECEM IACOBI ·I· MAGNÆ BRITANNIÆ REGIS TOTIVSQ ANGLICI CONVOCATI PARLEMENTI·

A contemporary sketch of the conspirators in the Gunpowder Plot.

been judges to my condemnation, we may yet hereafter in Heaven verily meet together, to our everlasting salvation.'

In the years that followed the trials of Fisher and More, Protector Somerset and his rival Northumberland, the Duke of Suffolk, Sir Thomas Wyatt, Thomas Howard, Duke of Norfolk, who tried to take Mary Queen of Scots as his fourth wife, Philip, Earl of Arundel, and Robert Devereux, Elizabeth's Earl of Essex, were all brought to trial, all condemned and all executed.

Indeed of all those brought to trial on charges of treason during this bloody century only one, Lord Dacre, was not judged guilty, and his trial in 1534 was before the holocaust, though that should not detract from his achievement, for, like all accused of treason, he was denied legal aid and it was only because he was able to defend himself, 'so manly, wittily and directly' that he was judged, 'not guilty', a verdict which occasioned enormous rejoicing in the City.

Perhaps the noblest figure after More to suffer during these troubled times was the Jesuit Priest, Edmund Campion. He refused to reveal the secrets of the Confessional, 'come rack or rope'. When he was sentenced he did not flinch. 'The only thing that we now have to say is that if our Religion do make us traitors we are worthy to be condemned; but otherwise are, and have been, as true subjects as ever the Queen had.'

The first of the great trials of the seventeenth century was that of the Gunpowder Plot conspiritors in January, 1606. It roused such enormous interest that special stands had to be erected inside the Hall and seats changed hands for as much as ten shillings each, though one Member of the Commons arrived to find his place occupied by someone 'of the baser sort', who had paid only fourpence for it.

In 1641 it was the turn of Thomas Wentworth, Earl of Strafford, and Charles I's Lord Lieutenant of Ireland, sacrificed by his Royal Master in a desperate attempt to appease his enemies. In an atmosphere tense with excitement and suspicion, 'Black Tom the Tyrant' was brought each day from the Tower with an escort of six barges. As with his sixteenth century predecessors in the Hall there was no chance of acquittal, but like most of them he met his end nobly. 'And now my Lords I thank God that I have been, by His blessing, sufficiently instructed in the extreme vanity of all temporary enjoyments compared to the importance of our eternal duration. And so my Lords, even so with all humility and all tranquillity of mind I submit clearly and freely to your judgement; and whether that righteous doom be to life or death, I shall repose myself, full of gratitude and confidence, in the arms of the great author of my existence. Te Deum laudamus'.

The trial was watched by Charles and by his Queen, Henrietta Maria, and by the young Prince of Wales, then a boy of ten. The King, when the verdict was announced, sought to save Strafford's life, promising either to imprison him or send him into exile. But the Lords passed the special Bill and Strafford lost his head by a majority of seven votes (twenty-six to nineteen), Charles himself signing the Bill after a few days of prevarication.

The execution of the conspirators in 1606.

Less than nine years later the most famous trial in English history, that of Charles himself, took place in the Hall. It was, of course, another 'show trial', but the certainty of the outcome did not detract from the significance or the solemnity of the proceedings. Even today it is those four short winter days in 1649 that first spring to mind whenever one walks through Westminster Hall.

The Court, 'in the name of the Commons in Parliament assembled and all the good people of England', was presided over by John Bradshaw, Chief Justice of Cheshire, an indifferent lawyer but a fanatical Puritan. He wore a bullet-proof hat, which is still preserved in the Taylorian Museum at Oxford, and sat on a crimson-covered chair. The proceedings opened with the roll call of the Commissioners. The first name called out was Lord Fairfax. The answer came from his wife sitting in the Gallery, 'Not here and never will be. He hath too much sense.'

The King, wearing a black suit and the blue ribbon of the Garter and carrying a white silver-topped cane, was seated in an armchair opposite Bradshaw, who informed him that the Commons, 'being sensible of the evils and calamities that have been brought upon this nation, and of the innocent blood that has been shed in it, which is fixed upon you as the principal author of it', has resolved by virtue of 'the fundamental power' vested in them to bring him to judgement. Just after the Solicitor-General, Cook, had opened the case a Scots woman, Lady Anna de Lille, the widow of a French Captain who had been in the King's service, called out that it was not the people who were making the accusations against their King but rebels and traitors. She was immediately seized, hot irons were sent for and she was branded on the shoulder and the head. 'His Majesty then seeing her flesh smoke and her hair all afire for him by their hot irons, much commiserated her and wished he could have been able to have requited her'.

The moment that the King was invited to address the Court the doors of the northern end of the Hall were opened and the crowds surged in, drowning his voice. When he could be heard he questioned by what authority they met. 'I have a trust committed to me by God by old and lawful descent. I will not betray that trust to answer a new and unlawful authority for all the world. Therefore let me know by what authority I have come hither and you shall hear more of me. Resolve me in that and I shall answer.' Bradshaw's reply was that their authority was 'of the Commons assembled in Parliament on behalf of the people of England, by which people you are elected King'.

Charles would have none of this. The Kingdom had been hereditary 'for near this thousand years'. He refused to plead or acknowledge the Court's authority and Bradshaw adjourned the Court until the following Monday to give time for 'the most obstinate man in Christendom' to change his mind. That the trial did not have the popular support Bradshaw claimed was shown by the cries of 'God bless him' and 'Justice' as the King was escorted away. During the

Thomas Wentworth, Earl of Strafford, being sentenced to death in Westminster Hall in 1641 — from an engraving by Wenceslas Hollar.

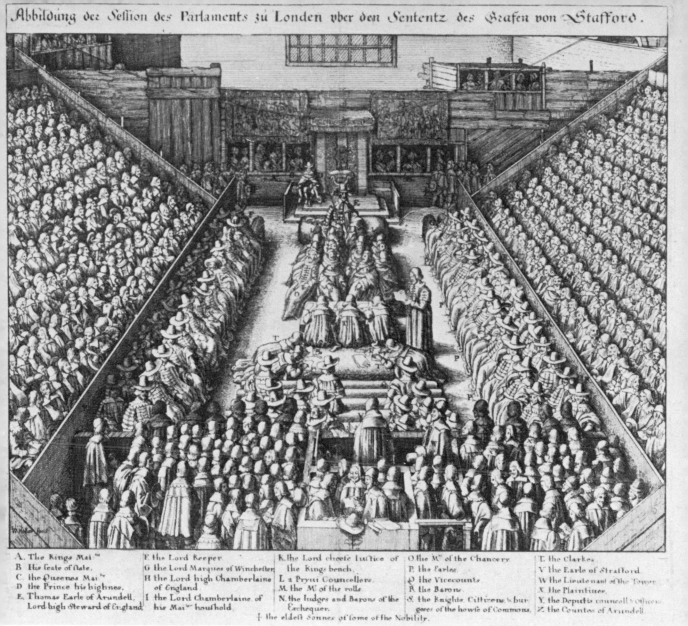

A. The Kings Ma.tie
B His feate of ftate.
C. the Queenes Ma.tie
D the Prince his highnes.
E. Thomas Earle of Arundell,
    Lord high Steward of England.

F. the Lord Keeper.
G the Lord Marquies of Winchefter
H the Lord high Chamberlaine
    of England
I the Lord Chamberlaine of
    his Ma.ties houfhold.

K the Lord chiefe Iuftice of
    the Kings bench.
L a Pryui Councellors.
M. the M.r of the rolls.
N. the Iudges and Barons of the
    Exchequer.

O the M.r of the Chancery.
P. the Earles.
Q the Vicecounts.
R the Barons.
S. the Knights Cittizens, & bur
    gores of the howfe of Commons.

T. the Clarkes.
V the Earle of Strafford.
W the Lieutenant of the Tower
X the Plaintines.
Y the Deputis councell & officers
Z the Countes of Arundell.

+ the eldeft fonnes of fome of the Nobility.

next day (Sunday) the Commissioners kept a fast in Whitehall and had to listen to sermons on the text, 'I will bind their Kings in chains and their nobles in fetters of iron.'

When the Court assembled on Monday the King was adamant. Asked to give a punctual and direct answer he said that he knew 'as much of the law as any gentleman in England and . . . I know I am pleading for the liberties of the people more than any of you . . . If power without law may make law, I do not know a subject in England who can be sure of his life or anything he can call his own.'

There were more shouts of 'God save the King' and then Colonel Hewson, the man who had wielded the branding iron on Saturday,

23

went over to the King and spat in his face, shouting out 'Justice! Justice! Upon the traitor!' Carefully wiping his cheek, the King remarked, 'Well sir, God hath justice in store for both you and me'.

The next day, Tuesday, Charles again refused to plead and was again acclaimed as he left the Hall. It was clear that he would never accept the authority of the Court and so, after lengthy deliberation, the Commissioners decided that the only thing for it was to summon the King before them and pass sentence. This they assembled to do on Saturday, 27 January. Charles was brought to the Bar but as Bradshaw rose the King spoke. 'I shall desire a word to be heard a little and I hope I shall have no occasion for interruption'. Bradshaw told him that he could answer in due time but that he must hear the Court first. Again the King tried to speak and Bradshaw repeated the set formula about the King being tried in the name of the people. At this Lady Fairfax interrupted the proceedings again, saying that not one quarter of the people would have agreed, 'Oliver Cromwell is a traitor'. Muskets were trained on her and her companion while Bradshaw rambled on. There was more wrangling and the King asked to be heard by the Lords and Commons, not in the Hall, but in the Painted Chamber. There was an adjournment to discuss this request, which was refused. Bradshaw then made an extraordinary speech, dredging up references to Sparta and the Roman Senate and reminding Charles, 'Parliaments were ordained to redress the grievances of the people'. Bradshaw called the Clerk to read the sentence which rehearsed all the alleged crimes of Charles and 'for all which treasons and crimes this Court does judge that the said Charles Stuart as a tyrant, traitor, murderer and public enemy to the good people of this nation, shall be put to death by severing his head from his body.'

Again the King tried to speak and again he was cut short, Bradshaw ordering, 'Guards, withdraw your prisoner'. As he turned away Charles exclaimed, 'I am not suffered for to speak. Expect what justice other people will have.' Two days later his head was held up for the multitudes to see 'amid a dismal and universal groan'.

After the Restoration the Hall continued to be used for major public trials. Undoubtedly the most unpleasant creature ever to be justly sentenced there was Titus Oates in 1685. He was fined 2,000 marks and the loss of his canonical habit on two charges of perjury. He was also put in the pillory outside the Hall and whipped from Newgate to Tyburn.

Three years later occurred the most celebrated Westminster Hall acquittal with the trial of the seven Bishops. Sancroft, Lloyd, Trelawny, Turner, Ken, White and Lake had refused to accept James II's Declaration of Indulgence,* and because they would not order it to be read in their dioceses they were brought to trial. Their acquittal sparked off enormous rejoicing and marked the beginning of the end of James II's brief and inglorious reign. Though there were some unpleasant scenes of mob violence amid the rejoicing, the Bishops were more worthy of public approbation and acclamation than the

Oliver Cromwell, Lord Protector of England, 1653–1658.

*Giving freedom of worship to Roman Catholics but feared by many as a prelude to the overthrow of the Established Church.

Two famous 18th-century figures tried in Westminster Hall. Left *Lord Lovat, the 'Fox of the North', condemned to death for his part in the Jacobite rebellion of 1745.* Right *Warren Hastings, whose trial spanned seven Parliamentary years between 1788 and 1795.*

next cleric to stand trial in the Hall, Dr Henry Sacheverell, impeached by the Whigs in 1710 for preaching a Tory sermon. Queen Anne came to his trial every day but his coach was as wildly cheered by the multitudes as was her sedan chair. We read of Tory ladies up before seven each morning to 'see and be seen at the trial', importuning young Lords of their acquaintance, 'to make a bustle to have their full number of tickets, eight-a-piece'. The Doctor had the lightest sentence ever administered at a major trial—he was suspended from preaching for three years: the Whigs obviously realized that they would have provoked a storm that they could not contain had he been more severely punished. When he did preach his next sermon it was to the Commons at St Margaret's, Westminster.

Five years later the 'Jacobite Lords' of the 1715 Rebellion were arraigned. Kenmure and Derwentwater went to the block. Lord Nithsdale was similarly sentenced but escaped owing to the courageous ingenuity of his wife who smuggled women's clothes into his cell in the Tower.

After the next Jacobite rising in 1745 came more rebel Lords, Cromarty, Kilmarnoch and Balmerino. All three were sentenced to death although Cromarty was later pardoned. The most famous of the Jacobite trials, however, was that of Lord Lovat, 'The Fox of the

North'. A cynical aplomb and macabre sense of humour remained with him to the last. The first witness, one of his servants, met with, 'How dare you, Sirrah, appear without your master's orders'. As he was led away to the inevitable sentence he turned to his judges, 'Farewell my Lords. We shall never meet again in the same place. I am sure of that.'

In 1760 Earl Ferrers was hanged at Tyburn with a silken rope after being convicted by his peers of murdering his steward. In 1756 another noble murderer William, Lord Byron, was sentenced to death for killing a man in a drunken brawl. He, however, was reprieved after claiming the privilege of peerage.

The two trials that dominated the headlines at the end of the century were markedly different from these. The first, in 1776, was of the Duchess of Kingston arraigned for bigamy. She seems to have enjoyed the experience. Mrs Pitt, one of the multitude of spectators at the trial, wrote to a friend, 'I am persuaded that the Duchess is not in the least degree humbled by her position, but mightily pleased with herself for having secured so brilliant a house. People fought and struggled for their places, just as for the Opera on a great night.' The whole trial was something of a farce, and by a suitably theatrical display of emotion at the right moment the Duchess managed to avoid the prescribed penalty of having her hand branded upon the block.

A very different trial was that of Warren Hastings which began in 1788 and occupied one hundred and forty-nine Parliamentary days spread over seven years. Fanny Burney, whose royal mistress, Queen Charlotte, gave her a day off to witness the opening of the trial has left a splendidly vivid description of the Hall. 'The whole of the green benches for the House of Commons occupied a third of the upper end of the Hall and the whole of the left side; to the right of us on the same level was the Grand Chamberlain's Gallery . . . The bottom (the south end of the Hall) contained the Royal Family's box and the Lord High Steward's, above which was a large gallery appointed for receiving company with Peers' tickets.' There was a gallery above the Commons' seats with the Duke of Newcastle's box and special accommodation for the Queen and the four eldest Princesses 'who were there incog, not choosing to appear in state'. Mrs Fitzherbert was in the royal box and among the other spectators on the opening day were Gibbon, Reynolds and Mrs Siddons. 'In the middle of the Hall was placed a large table and at the head of it was the seat for the Chancellor, and round it seats for the judges, the Masters in Chancery, the Clerks and all who belong to the law; the upper end and the right side of the room was allotted to the Peers in their robes; the left side to the Bishops and Archbishops. In the front of the Great Chamberlain's box was the place for the prisoner, with a box for his Council on the right, and on his left a box for the managers, or the committee, for the prosecution. These managers were led by Edmund Burke who 'held a scroll in his hand and walked alone, his brow knit with corroding care and deep labouring thought . . . Mr Fox followed next, Mr Sheridan,

The Coronation Banquet of James II, 1685.

Mr Windham, and Messrs Anstruther, Grey, Adam, Michael Angelo
Taylor, Pelham, Colonel North, Mr Frederick Montagu, Sir Gilbert
Elliot, General Bergoyne, Dudley Long, etc. They were all named over
to me by Lady Claremont or I should not have recollected even those
of my acquaintance from the shortness of my sight.' According to
Lady Claremont the Members of the House of Commons when they
took their seats looked 'so little like gentlemen and so much like
hairdressers'.

The indicted Hastings expressed himself, 'impressed, deeply
impressed. I come before your Lordships, equally confident in my own
integrity and in the justice of the Court before which I am to clear it.'
Clear it he did, but not for seven years: indeed he was virtually on trial
for ten years because it was two and a half years before the trial began
that Burke tabled a Motion in the House 'respecting the conduct of a
gentleman just returned from India'.

Hastings presented a sorry figure, frail and emaciated. 'What an awful moment this for such a man,' wrote Fanny Burney, 'a man fallen from such height of power to a situation so humiliating—from the most unlimited command of so large a part of the Eastern world to be cast at the feet of his enemies, of the great tribunal of his country, and of the nation at large, assembled thus in a body to try and judge him! Could even his prosecutors at that moment look on—and not shudder at least, if they did not blush?' Burke could. He was full of fanatical eloquence and incapable of conceiving any thoughts of charity as he launched the attack. 'I charge Warren Hastings in the name of the Commons of England here assembled, with high crimes and misdemeanours—I charge him with fraud and abuse, treachery and robbery! I charge him with cruelties unheard of and devastations almost without a name! . . . I impeach therefore, Warren Hastings, in the name of our holy religion which he has disgraced. I impeach him in the name of the English Constitution which he has violated and broken. I impeach him in the name of the Indian millions whom he has sacrificed to injustice. I impeach him in the name and by the best rights of human nature which he has stabbed to the heart and I conjure this High and Sacred Court to let not these pleadings be heard in vain.'

The trial dragged on. In the eighteenth century Parliament met for only a few months each year and even during the period of its meeting recesses were frequent, and, of course, the Commons had other business to transact. And so for seven long years Hastings remained on trial. His plight did excite considerable sympathy, a sympathy which increased with the years. Many of those who, like Boswell, got to know him came to like him. But for Burke there could be no compensating qualities. The crimes of Hastings are 'of the grovelling kind which do not usually grow upon a throne but are hatched upon dung hills'. He was 'a vulture battening upon carrion. He wallowed in his stye of infamy in the filth of disgrace; he fattened on the offals and excrements of dishonour.' This ranting produced such rejoinders as:

Lawyers stroll among the shops in Westminster Hall on their way to court, 1738.

> 'Oft have I wondered that on Irish ground,
> No poisonous reptiles ever yet were found,
> Reveal'd the secret stands of nature's work;
> She sav'd her venom to create a Burke'

Burke kept it up until the end. Though witnesses died and others returned to India he went on. Finally on 23 April, 1795, before an audience as large as the one that had gathered seven years before, the verdict was delivered. On each charge Hastings was acquitted, on some unanimously and on others by a large majority. 'Mr Hastings bowed respectfully and retired.' He retired a ruined man, for the trial had cost him almost one hundred thousand pounds. Burke's career was ruined too. Criticized in the House for turning the proceedings into a farce through his intemperance he applied for the Chiltern Hundreds. A year later he was dead.

Only one more man was to stand impeached in Westminster Hall.

In 1806 Henry Dundas, the first Viscount Melville, was charged with peculation, using public money for his own ends while Treasurer to the Navy. Impeachment itself had only been brought about by the casting vote of the Speaker, but that did not detract from the panoply of the occasion. Like Hastings, however, Melville was acquitted, and a year later he was restored to the Privy Council.

*   *   *   *

Though these trials, where there were no lives at stake, were enjoyed by a gossip-hungry society, as colourful social occasions, they did not compare for theatre, pageantry or disorder with those other memorable gatherings with which the Hall was most closely associated for many centuries: the Coronation Banquets. For almost

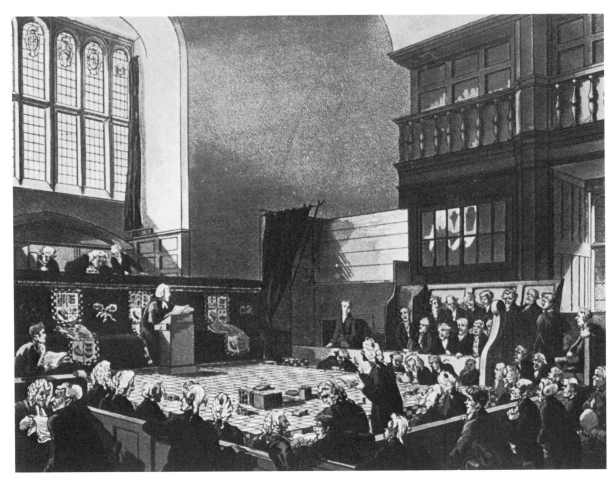

six hundred years almost every English Sovereign went to his Coronation from Westminster Hall and returned there to celebrate the event in suitable style. The first Coronation feast of which we have any record was that in which Henry II waited upon his own son, whom he insisted should be crowned in his (the father's) lifetime. We are told that this son, who in the event never succeeded to the throne (he died in rebellion against his father) haughtily disdained the royal homage paid to him. 'My father in doing it thinketh it not more than becometh him, he being born of princely blood only on the mother's side, and serveth me that am a King born, having both a King to my father and a Queen to my mother.'

Such behaviour did not mar either the Coronation banquet of Henry III's Queen Eleanor in 1236 nor the magnificent banquet held in honour of the Coronation of Edward I in 1274. We have some records of the provisions used to furnish the celebration tables on that occasion; 440 oxen and cows, 430 sheep, 430 pigs, 16 fat boars, 278 flitches of bacon, 460 capons, in addition to other game and poultry.

The Court of King's Bench, 1808.

Whilst the fountains outside 'poured forth white and red wine like
rainwater for those who would drink at pleasure,' the King of
Scotland, the Earls of Arundel, Gloucester, Pembroke and Warren
arrived, 'each having in their company one hundred illustrious
Knights wearing their Lord's armour, and when they alighted from
their palfreys they also set them free that whosoever chose might take
them unquestioned.'

Our medieval Kings spared no expense. We know that in the next
reign one thousand pipes of wine were brought from Bordeaux for the
Coronation, and that when Edward III was crowned one thousand
and fifty six pounds, nineteen shillings and threepence was spent on
adorning and decorating the Hall and Abbey.

At the Coronation of the boy Richard II in 1377 we have the first
record of the appearance of one of the most flamboyant and familiar
figures of later banquets, the King's Champion. A creation of the age
of chivalry, his duty was to enter the Hall at an appropriate moment
mounted on a white steed, and, throwing down his gauntlet,

challenge to mortal combat any who would question the King's right to the crown. An elaborate ritual and form of words was evolved. 'If any person, of what degree soever, high or low, shall gainsay our Sovereign Lord King . . . to be right heir to the Imperial Crown of this Realm, or that he ought not to enjoy the same, here is his champion who saith that he lieth and is a false traitor, being ready in person to combat with him; and in this quarrel will venture his life against him on what day soever shall be appointed.' Escorted by the High Constable of England and the Earl Marshal, the Champion had the challenge repeated three times by a Herald and then, if it was not answered—and it never was—the King would drink to the Champion from a gold cup. This was then handed to him as his fee. Throughout the centuries the office of King's Champion remained in the Dymoke family of Scrivelsby in Lincolnshire and to this day the head of the family has the right to carry the Royal Standard at the Coronation. Froissart gives us a particularly graphic account of the Coronation of Henry IV. He, no doubt, wished to make up in ostentation what he lacked in legitimacy, having just deposed Richard II. According to the chronicler, 'There were nine fountains continually flowing with red and white wine, independently of another fountain in the Palace court giving issue to similar liquids from various mouths. At the banquet itself, among the first course dishes were boar's head, swans, capons, pheasants, heron, sturgeons, in the second, venison in frumenty, jelly, young pigs, stuffed peacocks, cranes, venison paste, tongue, bittorn, "fowls gilded", large tarts, rashers of ham or brawn, and in the last, quinces, partridges, young eagles, curlews, pigeons, quails, snipes, small birds, rabbits, white brawn sliced, fritters, sweetmeats, eggs.' Between each course, and while Sir Thomas Dymoke, 'on a goodly steed, barbed with crimson housings' issued the customary challenge, 'subtleties' were served. These took the place of the Victorian 'between course sorbet' and were apparently made of pastry in the form of statuettes of the King's patron saint.

Over one hundred years later the Coronation of Henry VIII was marked with similar splendour. The Queen, Catherine of Aragon, was borne on a litter between two white palfreys 'in white satin embroidered, her hair hanging down her back to a very great length, beautiful and goodly to behold, and on her head a coronet set with many rich Orient stones.' The King gave another sumptuous feast for his next Queen, Anne Boleyn.

Not surprisingly the restored Charles II's Coronation was an especially glittering affair, and so was that of his brother James II. No doubt they wished to upstage the 'Happy Inauguration' of the Cromwellian régime which had also taken place in the Hall.

For the superstitious, however, James II's Coronation celebrations were marked by an unhappy omen. As he passed along the royal blue carpet from the Abbey to the Hall after the Coronation ceremony the crown tilted on his head and would have fallen off had not Henry

Sydney steadied it. 'This is not the first time,' Sydney remarked, 'that our family has upheld the Crown.'

The ceremonial observed at James II's Coronation became the model for succeeding ceremonies. One of the features that was particularly attractive, and eagerly repeated by those who had the arrangement of later processions, was the 'strewer of flowers in ordinary, to His Majesty'. Mary Dowell, assisted by six women, 'two to a basket, each basket containing six bushels', strewed sweet herbs and flowers in the way of the King as he walked from the Abbey to the Hall.

At the Coronation of George III and Queen Charlotte in 1761 there were a number of technical hitches. Before the crowning the regalia was laid out on the marble table in Westminster Hall and nobody seemed to know whose responsibility it was to carry it in the procession to the Abbey. At length the King and Queen set out accompanied by the Earl Marshal and other senior officers of state, and with the ancient Bishop of Lincoln 'dawdling by the side of the Queen'. Things at the Abbey were not much better for the long and involved ceremony had obviously not been rehearsed and many were kept waiting over six hours in Westminster Hall for the banquet to begin. When the King at last entered the chandeliers were lit, an event which, according to Thomas Gray the poet, caused some alarm. The method used to light them was to set fire to a train of flax along which the flames ran so swiftly that all the candles, and there were three thousand of them, were burning in half a minute. The Queen and her ladies 'were in no small terror'. Small wonder, for the flax fell in large flakes on the heads of those beneath. Fortunately no one was burned but in the erection of the chandeliers some of the workmen had, they boasted, 'broken the noses and cut off the ears of a whole legion of angels' — those wonderful figures carved four hundred years before.

There was another extraordinary incident when the King's Champion appeared. The Champion himself behaved admirably but not so his companions. One of them, Lord Talbot, had been so anxious to train his horse to back so that it would not turn its rump towards the King that the poor animal would not move forwards at all. It, therefore, entered the Hall rear first. There was such hilarity as a result that Horace Walpole reckoned it all 'a terrible indecorum'. When the King's Champion threw down the gauntlet a white kid glove fluttered down by its side. No one knew whence it came, but the rumour, to which Horace Walpole gave credence, grew that it had been flung down by Charles Edward, the Young Pretender, who had somehow managed to get himself into the Hall to witness the Coronation festivities.

While the banquet was proceeding the ladies who were sitting in the galleries above, ravenous with hunger, could not bear the sight of their husbands feasting below, and some of them formed ropes of handkerchiefs which they let down and hauled up with 'a chicken or a bottle of wine' attached to the end. It was an unorthodox way of staving off the pangs of hunger in such august surroundings, but at least they did rather better than the Knights of the Bath. They had been overlooked, 'no table was provided for them. An airy apology, however, was served to them instead of a substantial dinner.'

It was ten o'clock before the King and Queen retired and then the great doors of the Hall were thrown open according to custom and the throng immediately 'cleared it of all the moveables such as the victuals, plates, cloths, dishes, etc. and in short everything that would stick to their fingers'.

Though both George VI and Queen Elizabeth II gave post-Coronation lunches for Commonwealth guests in Westminster Hall, the last traditional Coronation banquet to be held was that of George IV on 19 July, 1821. Those in charge of the ceremonies were determined that they would be more decorously managed than they had been for his father.

In order to remove the Court of King's Bench to prepare the Hall a special Act of Parliament was duly passed. However, the lawyers who were due to appear were not told and there are entertaining accounts of a host of dishevelled Barristers rushing to the Guildhall, many losing their wigs in the stampede.

Special wooden flooring was put down and on the royal platform a throne was erected, nineteen feet high and seven feet wide, covered with crimson velvet and forming a shrine for the royal chair which was adorned with the royal arms, embroidered in the most costly style.

There was such a run on the tailors of London that they could not supply court dress to everyone who wanted it, and so recourse was made to theatrical costumiers and in the end there were some bizarre spectacles: lawyers turned up in military uniform and city merchants 'in the sombre canonicals of the divine'. Some of those who had tickets arrived as early as three o'clock in the morning. The artist Benjamin Robert Haydon gives us a splendid description of the entry of the King some eight hours later. 'Something rustles, and a being buried in satin, feathers and diamonds rolls gracefully to his seat. The room rises with a sort of feathered silken thunder, plumes wave, eyes sparkle, glasses are out and mouths smile and one man becomes the prime object of attraction to thousands. The way in which the King bowed was really royal. As he looked towards the Peeresses and foreign Ambassadors, he showed like some gorgeous bird of the East'. The procession formed up and went towards the Abbey, headed by Miss Fellows and her herb women and 'the sounding of trumpets and the beating of drums'.

Five hours later the newly crowned King returned to the Hall after a ceremony somewhat marred by the undignified spectacle of his estranged Queen vainly seeking entry to the Abbey. The candles were lit and such was the heat that 'several of the ladies fainted and the superb dresses of the Peers and Peeresses were spoiled by the profuse globules of melted wax which were continually falling upon them; and to increase their embarrassment, an escape was impossible from

Fighting the Fire, from a contemporary anonymous drawing, 1834.

the place where their unlucky destiny had placed them. If a lovely female dared to raise her look to discover from what quarter the unwelcome visitation came, she was certain of receiving an additional patch upon her cheek, which, in order to disencumber herself of, obliged her to wipe away also the roseate hue which had been imparted to her countenance at her toilet.'

Understandably the King had a rest before taking his seat at the table and there was a further delay in serving the meal when it was discovered that despite all the Coronation plate the royal table lacked soup ladles, spoons and carvers. Soon, however, the King's Champion came riding in, on a horse which had been hired from Astley's circus. In spite of the training it had obviously received there it was noticeably agitated by the shouts of acclamation that greeted the challenges.

Never can so much food have been consumed in the Hall: 7,442 lbs beef; 7,133 lbs veal; 2,474 lbs mutton; 20 quarters of house lamb; 20 legs of house lamb; 5 saddles of lamb; 55 quarters of grass lamb; 160 lamb sweetbreads; 389 cow heels; 400 calves' feet; 250 lbs suet; 160 geese; 720 poulets and capons; 1,160 chickens; 520 fowls for stock; 1,730 lbs bacon; 550 lbs lard; 912 lbs butter; 84 hundred eggs; not to mention 160 tureens of soup, 160 dishes of fish; 160 dishes of shellfish; 80 of venison; 160 of vegetables; 640 pastries; 400 of creams and jellies; 480 boats of sauces. The assembled company consumed 100 bottles of Champagne, 20 dozen of Burgundy; 200 dozen of claret; 50 dozen of hock; 50 dozen Mosel; 50 dozen Maderia; 350 dozen of port and sherry. There were one hundred gallons of iced punch and one hundred barrels of ale and porter. 6,794 plates were used, 1,406 soup plates and 1,499 dessert plates. In all the Coronation—and the banquet must have accounted for a large share in it—cost £243,390.6s.2d.—without the royal robes!

Again the food was passed to the ladies in the gallery but as soon as the King retired decorum went to the winds and there was a mass

Mr Gladstone lying in state in Westminster Hall, 1898.

assault on what was left. Not satisfied with demolishing the food in a manner in which 'the distinction of sex and almost all the common rules of politeness seem to have been forgotten' the assembly then turned their attention to the table ornaments. There was hardly a knife or fork that was not carried off as a souvenir. Everything but the pewter had been removed from the royal table, but everything bore the royal cipher and so was highly prized.

The crowds outside were kept back with considerable difficulty otherwise there would have been 'a scene of indiscriminate plunder'. As it was the persons of quality who had attended were, by the end of the proceedings, 'in a complete state of exhaustion . . . All the ordinary punctilios of society were of necessity forgotten. Peers and Peeresses, Judges and Privy Councillors, Knights of all Orders and commoners of all degrees were alike worn out by fatigue and lay promiscuously, some on sofas, some on chairs, and a still greater number on the matted floor of the rooms and passages in which they happened to have sought refuge. Many, while in this situation, were overtaken by sleep, and in this happy state of forgetfulness, scenes were presented extremely at variance with the splendid spectacle which had been but a few hours before exhibited.'

William IV and Queen Victoria decided not to repeat the performance after their Coronations.

During the nineteenth century, however, the Hall continued to play a prominent part in the nation's life. It was still very much a public meeting place. The law courts moved out of the Hall itself in 1824 when Sir John Soane's new Courts had been completed, but these opened out of the Hall and indeed the whole west side was occupied by a series of court rooms with seven doors leading into the Hall through openings cut in the original wall erected in the reign of William Rufus. At the same time the walls of the Hall were refaced on the inside and the carvings on the corbels restored. The floor too — the Hall had been flooded in 1818 — was relaid with York stone.

The Law Courts remained here until the completion of the new Palace of Justice in the Strand in 1884 and so for most of the nineteenth century Westminster Hall remained the centre of the legal universe and the scene of legal ceremonies as on the first day of term when the Lord Chancellor and the judges, after taking breakfast in the Hall of Lincoln's Inn, came in procession to Westminster Hall.

When Sir Charles Barry (who will feature prominently in these pages) came to create the new Palace he was anxious that Westminster Hall should be one of its focal points. He had rather extravagant ambitions for its transformation. His son tells us, in his biography of his father, that 'Frescoes, trophies and statues were to have met the eye, set in a profuse enrichment of colour and mosaic and the whole was to have formed a British Valhalla. "I would propose," Barry said, "that Westminster Hall should be made the depository, as in former times, for all trophies obtained in wars with foreign nations. These trophies might be so arranged above the paintings on the walls and in the roof as to have a very striking and interesting effect. I would further suggest that pedestals, twenty in number, answering to the position of the principal ribs of the roof should be placed so as to form a central avenue thirty feet in width from the north entrance door to St Stephen's Porch, for statues of the most celebrated British statesmen whose services may be considered by Parliament to merit a similar tribute to their memories".' In a letter to *The Times* he strenuously denied that he had proposed to raise the roof, although that was a suggestion seriously advanced by others at a later date.

Mercifully, however, his plans were not adopted in any particular, although the Hall was used to display the designs sent in by competing artists for the various frescoes with which the new Palace was to be decorated. During one such exhibition three hundred thousand people tramped through the Hall in six weeks.

The only significant change effected during the building of the new Palace came about as the result of the construction of St Stephen's Hall on the site of the old Chamber of the Commons. This now formed a corridor between St Stephen's Entrance and the great Central Lobby and to accommodate it Barry moved back the great south window of the Hall and built the two large and imposing flights of steps which, with a great platform dividing them, have served as the stage for great ceremonies this century.

When Soane's Law Courts were demolished and the lawyers moved out, it had to be decided how the Norman work along the great west wall could best be preserved. After considerable disputes between various architectural experts, the present arrangements which Pearson, the leading Gothic architect of the day, reckoned would be most consistent with the original scheme of things, was decided upon and a double cloister-like structure was erected housing various Parliamentary offices and a new Grand Committee Room.

The end of the nineteenth century saw the Hall put to a new, solemn, and wholly appropriate use—the use with which many this century most closely associate it. In 1898 Mr Gladstone died and his body lay in state in the Hall. 'Brought in the early morn from Hawarden Castle to Westminster, the remains of the aged Statesman were received by His Grace the Duke of Norfolk, the Earl Marshal, attended by the officers at Arms and the Chaplain of the House of Commons . . . The coffin was placed in the centre of the Hall, upon a raised bier, on the foot of which was a white silk pall embroidered with gold and bearing the inscription, '*Requiescat in Pace*'—the pall a gift to Mr Gladstone by the Armenians, whose cause he had so stoutly championed. With touching simplicity the arrangements were carried out. No flowers or decorations were placed in the Hall; no ostentatious emblems of woe figured in the picture. At the corners of the bier four massive silver candlesticks with candles were placed, and at the head of the coffin stood an elaborate embossed brass cross brought from St John's Church, Westminster. From sunset to dawn

The Queen attends the celebrations to mark the 700th anniversary of Parliament in 1965.

38

relays of clergy maintained a solemn vigil.'

For the two days that Gladstone lay there nearly a quarter of a million people slowly filed by; 'Class distinctions were obliterated in the general desire to pay this last tribute to the illustrious dead.' In the throng were 'Peers and legislators, judges and great church dignitaries, sharing their common sorrow with the artisan in his working clothes, the policeman off duty and the soldier in uniform . . . The scene presented one of extreme solemnity and impressiveness, and the eye ranged over a great mass of people coming in from New Palace Yard and moving slowly along, all turning their heads reverently towards the coffin when passing, and many exhibiting signs of emotion, the while an awed silence prevailed, broken only by the rustling movement of many feet.'

Those sounds were to be echoed many times this century. In 1910 Edward VII lay where Gladstone had lain. On 10 October, 1930, forty-eight coffins containing those who were killed in the disastrous crash of the R 101 airship were placed there. In 1936 the nation paid homage to George V, and in 1952 his son, George VI, lay in state.

Perhaps the most moving of all such occasions came in January, 1965, when the honour that had been accorded to Gladstone was given to Sir Winston Churchill. A million people filed by in thankful, silent tribute to the greatest Parliamentarian of the twentieth century, and one of the greatest leaders this country has ever known.

All the ceremonies held in the Hall during this century have not been solemn ones. In 1923 George V came to mark the completion of eight years restoration work on the majestic roof, and in 1935 he was back again, this time to receive Loyal Addresses from the faithful Lords and Commons to mark his Silver Jubilee. In 1937, six thousand Canadian pilgrims returned from Vimy Ridge and were addressed by Baldwin, and in 1939, just six months before the outbreak of war, Lebrun, the President of the French Republic, addressed the Lords and Commons as his great successor, De Gaulle, was to do twenty years later.

The most colourful and moving ceremony of recent years was the presentation of Loyal Addresses on the occasion of another Silver Jubilee, this time that of Queen Elizabeth II. As when her grandfather was acclaimed, the Lord Chancellor led Lords and Commons in three rousing cheers for the monarch. There must have been some present on that cold May day in 1977 who remembered the earlier ceremony and the words of George V, perhaps the most appropriate spoken at any ceremony in the Great Hall, 'Beneath these rafters of medieval oak, silent witnesses of historic tragedies and pageants, we celebrate the present under the spell of the past.'

CHAPTER TWO

The Old Palace—
from Birth to Destruction

The Parliament of Edward I—the earliest illustration of a King meeting with Lords and Commons.

O N that October morning one hundred and one years earlier those with a sense of history must have felt that the spell of the past had been broken. The great Hall still stood but the rest of the Palace had seen and suffered its final tragedy.

The mob may have cheered as the walls of Westminster crumbled but among those who cherished Parliamentary traditions and valued great buildings there was a sense of deep loss, even though, as the Sunday papers pointed out, there was general agreement that the old Palace of Westminster had been ill-fitted to house the Parliament of a great nation.

Certainly it had never been designed for that purpose. Indeed there had been little design about the Palace at all. It was an odd, rambling assortment of buildings, a veritable warren of a Palace, haphazardly assembled over the centuries at the whim of kings or to meet the needs of the legislators who gradually took it over.

There was, however, no more hallowed spot in the Kingdom. We first read of it as Thorney Island—the Isle of Thorns—in the pages of the old Saxon chronicles. Then it was a forlorn and dank spot and in the oldest documentary references it is designated '*in loco terribili*', although as early as the eighth century there was an important monastery there.

Canute was the first King to make Thorney his home and by the time of his death in 1035 Westminster was the principal Royal residence. Canute's wooden Palace was burnt down but when Edward the Confessor came to the throne in 1042 he rebuilt it. His greatest ambition, fulfilled on the very eve of his death, was to build a great Abbey at Westminster and so he rarely left the place from which he could supervise its construction. There he received William of Normandy, and there in 1066 he died.

William himself took up residence at Westminster after the conquest and for the next four and a half centuries it was the greatest of the royal palaces. As we have seen, his son, William Rufus, was responsible for the building of Westminster Hall and almost all later Kings left their mark.

The last King to live there was Henry VIII, but a fire destroyed much of the palace in 1512 and after that Henry spent little time there. On Wolsey's fall from grace in 1530 he finally left Westminster and moved into the Cardinal Archbishop's grander residence at York

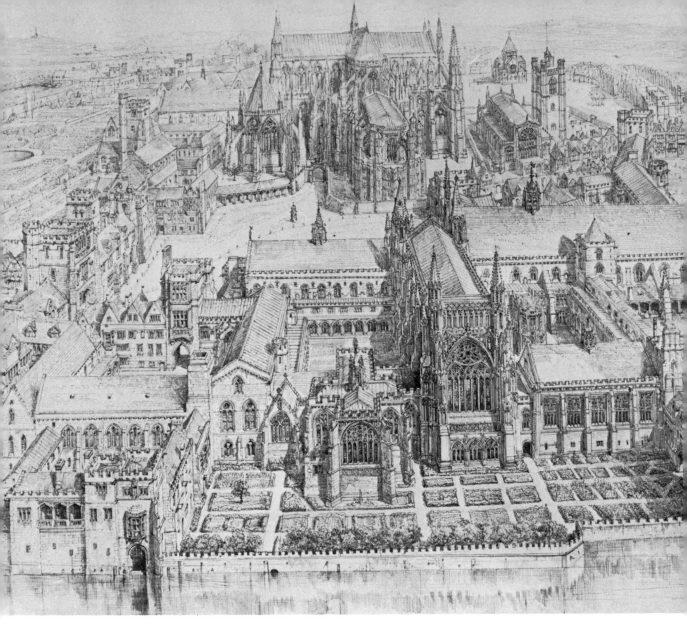

House a few hundred yards away—renaming it Whitehall.

Though Westminster's 'parliamentary connection' might be said to have begun with the Great Council which William the Conqueror held there in 1076, in those early days, where the King was the Court was, and the first true Parliament, representative of all the estates of the Realm, was summoned by De Montfort in 1265. The practice of summoning the Commons was firmly established after Edward I's Model Parliament in 1295 but it was not until 1377 that the two Houses began the practice of sitting separately.

For almost two hundred years after that when a Parliament was summoned (and meetings were neither frequent nor regular) the Commons met in the Chapter House of the Abbey. It was only after the

The Palace of Westminster in the reign of Henry VIII—an artist's reconstruction.

upheavals of the Reformation that Henry VIII's son, the young and sickly Edward VI, in 1547 made over the collegiate Chapel of St Stephen within the Palace of Westminster to the Commons for their meeting place. This was the Chamber—the Chamber of Hampden and Pym, of Walpole and the Pitts, of Fox and Burke, of the Grand Remonstrance and the great Reform Bill—that was destroyed on 16 October, 1834.

St Stephen's Chapel had been built originally by King Stephen in honour of his martyred namesake but of the twelfth century structure there was no trace, for the Chapel had been completely rebuilt during the reigns of the three Edwards. On its completion it was one of the two most beautiful apartments in the Palace.

It was a two-storeyed building designed by Michael of Canterbury, a master mason of consummate skill. The structure was completed in 1350 and was already a place of great beauty with statues of angels standing on brackets of Purbeck marble in niches round the walls. For over a decade after, craftsmen, under the direction of Master Hugh of St Albans, worked to beautify the interior with splendid paintings. The account books of the period are full of details of their activities and contain lists of the materials they used; pigs' bristles, squirrels' tails, goose, swan and peacock feathers, gold foil, silver, vermilion, verdigris, red and white lead and ochre.

Finally completed in 1363, the Chapel must have presented a dazzling spectacle. At the east end was a representation of the Adoration of the Magi with the kneeling figures of St George and King Edward III and Queen Philippa and their ten sons and daughters. Along the north and south walls, in rows of rectangular panels, were pictures depicting the story of Job and other biblical subjects. Between the panels every available space was enriched with decoration— royal lions and fleur-de-lys, the arms of the royal family, angels, doves, eagles and exotic creatures.

This was the Chapel into which the Commons moved and it remained essentially unaltered, though no doubt not universally appreciated by those who used it, until in 1692 Sir Christopher Wren was charged with the task of making it more suitable as a debating chamber. He tackled the job with great thoroughness, having the clerestory removed, the roof lowered, and the east front altered to incorporate classic windows and turrets. All the pictures were covered and all the stained glass taken out. The seating arrangements continued to follow the old collegiate chapel design of stalls facing each other across the aisle, Mr Speaker's chair occupying the position of the former altar.

A few years later more changes were made in order to make room for the forty-five new Scottish Members, following the Act of Union in 1707, and again in 1801, following the union with Ireland and the disappearance of the Dublin Parliament, another hundred Members had to be accommodated.

At this time Wren's panelling was removed and the wall paintings

revealed in almost pristine condition, only to be destroyed to make way for two extra rows of benches to seat the Irish—though fortunately not before they had been faithfully copied. Just over thirty years later the destruction of St Stephen's Chapel was complete and all we have to remind us of its former glory is a series of watercolour drawings still in the Palace collection.

Another remarkable and renowned apartment of the Old palace was the Painted Chamber. Originally part of the Norman Palace, it too had been renovated and redecorated at the height of the Court School of Painting during the reign of Edward III, and was, with St Stephen's, soon recognized as one of the wonders of Europe. Not even the thirteenth century wall paintings at Winchester rivalled those of the Painted Chamber. The subjects were mainly of Old Testament derivation. The side walls were divided into tiers and painted with scenes of bloodshed, martyrdom, warfare and destruction, whilst the corner of the north wall surrounding an opening into an Oratory was covered with a huge painting of the Coronation of Edward the Confessor. Angels were everywhere and there was a series of seven-foot high virtues triumphing over vice. The floor was beautifully tiled and the ceiling covered with carved and painted bosses. Though the name remained, as in St Stephen's Chapel the paintings disappeared, covered with whitewash, paper and tapestries, until revealed during the major reconstruction of 1800. Here again, meticulous copies were made and a hundred years later Professor Tristram was able to create some magnificent replicas which now hang, not to particular advantage, on the darkened stairs that lead down to the Terrace of the House of Commons.

It was a very happy chance that these early nineteenth century renovations took place because it meant that the entire Palace was surveyed in detail. We have plans showing, for example, the exact site of the cellar where the conspirators hid their gunpowder in 1605. But plans are all we have for, with the exception of the Great Hall, the Crypt and some of the cloisters, nothing survives of the Old Palace except the little Jewel Tower hard by the Abbey on the far side of Old Palace Yard. And, as we have seen, although some documents were salvaged, and some of the portraits and furniture from the Speaker's House, most of the original contents of the Palace perished. Wall paintings, sculptures, glass, the famous tapestries presented to Elizabeth I depicting the defeat of the Armada: all were lost.

To get an idea of the Old Palace and of the great events that took place there, we must rely on the documents that do remain, and on the drawings and prints which have come down to us. The earliest picture we have of Parliament at work in Westminster shows Edward I presiding over the Estates of the realm with considerable ceremony. On his right, and on a lower seat, is Alexander, King of Scotland, on his left Llewellyn, Prince of Wales. At the side of King Alexander, one rung lower still, is the Archbishop of Canterbury, and below Llewellyn sits the Archbishop of York. On a woolsack, prominent in the centre of

The Painted Chamber as it was in 1807.

45

the picture, sit the Chancellor, the two Chief Justices and the Baron of the Exchequer. There are two other woolsacks with four men on each and they, no doubt, constitute the judicial bench. On the King's right are the Bishops, the Lords Spiritual, and to his left the other Peers. Occupying a 'cross bench' in front of the Bishops are a group accompanied by a black-robed individual with a chain around his neck, possibly an early 'Speaker', with some of the faithful Commons, although there is no record of anyone holding the office in Edward's reign. However, though the original drawing obviously dates from considerably later than Edward's death in 1307 and is therefore not entirely reliable it is the most authentic representation we have of a medieval Parliament. There is no evidence of a female presence, although in the reign of Edward I the Abbesses of Shaftesbury, Barking, St Mary, Winchester, and Wilton each received a summons to attend, as did a number of prominent noblewomen in the reign of Edward III. Apparently peeresses were allowed to be represented by proxy until the whole custom of female representation fell into disuse.

Of even shorter duration was the custom of summoning the 'Proctors of the Inferior Clergy'. They seceded from the Parliamentary assembly, preferring to meet the financial demands of the Crown in their provincial convocations. It was to meet those financial demands

The House of Commons and the House of Lords as they were before 1834.

Henry VIII meets his Parliament.

that the early Parliaments were summoned but though their meeting at all was of considerable constitutional significance, the truth was that with a strong sovereign there was little that Parliament, and especially the lower estates, could do to assert any power.

This was the main reason why the people's representative, 'admitted on suffrance to the company of his betters to aid, in spasmodic and ill-defined fashion, in ministering to the material needs of his Sovereign', did not have a position that was eagerly sought. Indeed with local interests claiming much of his time and roads that were bad and dangerous, where they existed at all, many a Burgess or Knight of the Shire went very unwillingly to Westminster.

He was, however, paid for his pains. In the middle of the fifteenth century most Members were receiving two shillings a day and by the reign of Henry VIII it was generally five shillings for each day spent either in attendance in Parliament or travelling to and fro. Some towns were even more generous to their representatives, though many were no more eager than the Members themselves about Westminster representation. Richard II and Edward III, for instance, both granted absolution from representation to certain areas as a mark of favour, or out of consideration for the poverty of the county or borough concerned.

Where representation was not excused the duties had to be performed if the wages were to be paid. We learn of Knights of Oxfordshire and Gloucestershire having their wages disallowed 'because they neglected their work', and there is evidence that these strict conditions were still imposed at the time of Henry VIII when it was decreed that 'No Members have writs to levy their expenses but those who staid to the end of the session, such only excepted who had licence to depart, who should have their expenses down to the time of departure provided they returned to the performance of their duties.'

The practice of paying Members declined during the following century and barely survived the Civil War. The last recorded case of payment, and this is an isolated one, dated from 1681 and refers to one Thomas King who sat for Harwich and who successfully sued the Borough for arrears of salary. While Members were paid they were also liable to fines for slack attendance. Even Members of the Lords were not absolved here, though most of the records of punishment seem to relate to Members of the Lower House.

As the Commons became regarded not so much as a convenience but as an integral part of Parliament, properly elected and with its own Chamber, so membership became regarded as less of a burden and more of an honour, though often a somewhat uncomfortable one. By the time Henry VI came to the throne Parliament had become an established part of the government of the land, its highest court and yet possessing features which no inferior court could boast, for it was also an assembly representative of all men, and to whose acts every man was therefore party.

Even after their move from the Chapter House of the Abbey to the

47

Palace the Commons, as today, did not have a Chamber to rival that of the Lords. There are frequent references to the 'great disproportions of the two Houses' in the Old Palace. Just before the fire the House of Lords, 'though having only four hundred, not more than two hundred of whom generally attended, was larger than the House of Commons where, of six hundred and fifty-eight Members, four hundred were supposed likely to attend'.

The Lords, too, was a more noble and imposing hall and had 'an aristocratic air breathing through every part of it'. At the upper end was the King's throne, surmounted by a rich canopy and drapery of crimson and gold. Before it was the woolsack, or seat of the Lord High Chancellor as first legal dignitary of the Realm, keeper of the King's conscience and Speaker of the House of Lords. The side benches were arranged, as in the House of Commons, facing each other and rising in elevation as they receded, but in place of the open floor in the centre there were cross benches. A visitor in the seventeenth century writes: 'The sub-division of parties in their Lordships' House were as follows: the King's Ministers sat on the right of the woolsack, or Speaker's chair, the Opposition occupied the benches on the left. The Independents, neutrals or indifferents, for there are some of each, usually seated themselves on the cross benches between the two. There being no side galleries the lofty side walls exhibited to great advantage the Armada tapestry; and the hall being well lighted, the benches covered with bright crimson cloth and the floor softly matted, the whole breathed an air of dignified repose and tranquillity that was appropriate to the place.'

In spite of the elegance of the Lord's Chamber, however, interest and attention increasingly focused on the Commons after they transferred to the Chapel of St Stephen. Not that the early days in St Stephen's were great days. In the reign of Elizabeth the Commons behaved more like a servile assembly than a group of independent-minded men. Queen Elizabeth treated them with lofty disdain. For instance when Parliament begged her to marry she gave a fairly gracious answer on the first occasion but on the second she told them, 'She was not surprised at the Commons, they had small experience and acted like boys. But that the Lords should have gone along with them, she confessed, had filled her with wonder'. Many of her utterances show that she had a nice contempt for the elected Chamber. 'I have, in the Assembly found such dissimulation where they have always professed plainness, that I marvel thereat. Yea, two faces under one hood and the body rotten . . . Henceforth beware how you prove your Prince's patience as you have done mine now.'

There were those like Peter Wentworth who did not take kindly to the obsequiousness of the House and the growing intemperance of the Queen. He soon found himself in the Tower and when the Queen graciously condescended to let him out after a month the Commons hardly knew how to express themselves in words fulsome enough to show their appreciation of the Queen's magnanimity.

Queen Elizabeth I in Parliament.

QUEEN ELIZABETH IN PARLIAMENT

A Ld Chanceller B Marquifes Earles & C Barons D Bifhops E Iudges F Mafters of Chancery G Clerks H Speaker of ẙ Commons
I Black Rod K Serieant at Armes L Members of the Commons houfe M Sʳ Francis Walſingham Secretary of State.

49

The Elizabethan Commons was not entirely servile. It did enact some important measures, laying the foundations for the administration of the Poor Law for the next three centuries, and attempting to grapple with the problem of maintaining the highways and with the administration of charities. It began, too, to flex its muscles in so far as its own composition was concerned, asserting its power to control its own affairs and establishing the right of the Commons to deal with contested election returns. Had Elizabeth been a less dominating and successful ruler it is certain that the Commons would have given her far more trouble and voiced far more criticism, for within a few years Members were taking on the whole might and majesty of the Crown, though it was a crown worn by a less imposing head.

There can have been few who poked around the smouldering ruins of St Stephen's Chapel on that October morning in 1834 who did not reflect on the great events that had taken place in that Chamber two hundred years before. Trouble had begun almost as soon as James I came south to succeed the great Queen, and Parliament's relations with that strange monarch, 'the wisest fool in Christendom' or, as another had it, 'God's silly vassal', were always strained.

The most memorable clash was in 1621. The King had had Sir Edwin Sandys committed to prison for remarks made in the course of debate. The House challenged the King's right to arrest. The King back-tracked to a degree, claiming that Sandys had not been arrested because of his speech, whilst at the same time seeking to assert his right, 'to punish any man's misdemeanours in Parliament as well during their sitting as after'. A declaration was entered in the *Journal* of the House affirming 'that the liberties, franchises, privileges, and jurisdiction of Parliament are the ancient and undoubted birthright and inheritance of the subjects of England; and that the arduous and urgent affairs concerning the King, State and defence of the realm and of the Church of England, and of the making and maintenance of laws and redress of mischiefs and grievances which daily happen within this Realm, are proper subjects and matter of council and debate in Parliament, and that in the handling and prosecuting of those businesses, every Member of the House hath, and of good right ought to have, freedom of speech to propound, treat, reason, bring to conclusion the same; that the Commons in Parliament have like liberty and freedom to treat of those matters in such order as in their judgement shall seem fittest; and that every Member of the said House hath like freedom from all impeachment, imprisonment, and molestation (other than by censure of the House itself) for or concerning any Bill, speaking, reasoning or declaring of any matter or matters touching the Parliament or Parliamentary business; and that if any of the said Members be complained of and questioned for anything said or done in Parliament, the same is to be showed to the King by the advice and assent of all the Commons assembled, before the King give credence to any private information.'

This clear and forthright expression of the rights of Parliament,

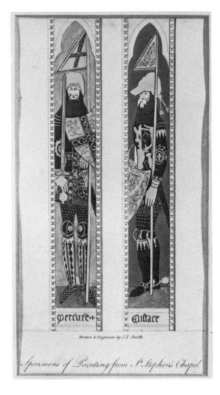

Specimens of Painting from St Stephen's Chapel

Specimen of Painting from St Stephen's Chapel

A series of reconstructions of wall paintings in St Stephen's Chapel from drawings by Thomas Smith, 1807.

drawn up by Coke, Glanville and other prominent Members, provoked fierce anger and resentment. James insisted that the House adjourn and ordered that the *Journal* be brought to Whitehall. There, he tore the offending page from the *Journal* and, 'His Majesty did . . . in full assembly of his Council and in the presence of the Judges, declare the said Protestation to be invalid, annulled, void and of no effect'. To this day the mutilated *Journal* is one of the proudest possessions of the House of Commons.

James had not finished. He issued a tetchy proclamation denouncing those 'ill-tempered spirits and ill-effected and discontented persons' who had presumed to express 'in any unseasonable hour of the day and a very thin House' their liberties, and Coke and Sir Robert Phillips soon found themselves committed to the Tower. Selden, Pym and Mallory were imprisoned elsewhere and another three of the malefactors exiled.

These despotic actions achieved the desired aim in the short term. For the rest of his reign James was untroubled by any form of Parliamentary outburst or challenge to the Royal Prerogative.

But the questions raised had not been solved and the new King, Charles I, was hardly of a disposition to solve them. Had his elder brother, Henry, not died in 1612 perhaps England would have escaped the upheaval of constitutional conflict and civil war. But Charles was incapable of coming to terms with the aspirations, still less the demands, of a Parliament that wanted a fundamental place in the constitution.

His unhappy combination of insensitivity and ineptitude together with his conviction of his own infallibility soon brought him into conflict with his faithful Commons. He had been on the throne for scarcely a year before he was involved in a fierce argument over Parliament's right to question the conduct of his favourite, Buckingham. Parliament wanted to impeach the Duke for mismanaging the Cadiz expedition. Charles refused to countenance any such criticism and had Eliot and Digges, the two Members most prominent in drawing up articles of impeachment, arrested. No royal action could have been more carefully calculated to provoke the fury of the House. Charles released the Members but dissolved the Parliament.

The events leading up to the complete severing of relations and the outbreak of civil war have been told too often to bear detailed repetition here but the Chamber of the Commons was the scene of the most significant and stirring events that led to the final break.

In these events farce as well as drama played a part—the Parliamentary buffoon is not unique to the twentieth century. At the height of the earnest discussions which led to the drawing up of the Petition of Right by the Parliament Charles summoned in 1628, a bizarre incident occurred when one Sir James Nethersole suddenly rose and asked leave to tell the House about the dream he had had during the night. There was a fair amount of hilarity at the request but Nethersole replied that 'Kingdoms have been saved by dreams'. A

somewhat bemused and tolerant House allowed him to continue for a time while he meandered on about a sheep and a bell-wether trying to cross a stream. He drew no moral but he did provoke the indignant protests of Eliot and others who thought that such idle and inconsequential nonsense should play no part in the deliberations of a great Assembly.

The Petition was drawn up and its passing took its place, with the sealing of the Magna Carta, as one of the most significant steps in the evolution of our constitution. This was the document that demanded, 'that no man hereafter be compelled to make or yield any gift, loan, benevolence, tax or such like charge, without common consent by Act of Parliament.'

Presented with the Petition, Charles prevaricated. Eventually he accepted it in the form of a Bill but shortly afterwards he prorogued Parliament.

Eliot and his colleagues were hardly satisfied and at the beginning of the new session began again to question the legality of some of the King's methods of raising revenue. The Speaker of the day, Sir John Finch, was very much a royal creature and had to be held in his Chair whilst a remonstrance against the King's arbitrary use of fiscal power was read by Eliot. This was too much for Charles who dissolved Parliament and imprisoned Eliot, Selden, Strode, Holles and others. This was no mere eight-day arrest. Eliot died in prison, Selden remained there for over four years and Parliament itself did not meet again for another eleven. During the 'eleven years tyranny' through which Charles ruled without reference to Westminster he built up a burning resentment which was bound to have explosive expression.

The first Parliament summoned in 1640, known as the 'Short Parliament', lasted barely three weeks before it became clear that the subject of grievances was to be raised again and that it would indeed dominate debate. However, with an empty exchequer and a Scottish army invading, even Charles could not manage indefinitely without Parliament, and so in November, 1640, the Parliament which was to become known as the 'Long Parliament' met. It was a Parliament 'which many before that time thought would have no beginning and afterwards that it would never have an end'.

It was hardly chastened or subservient. Its first action was to pass a Bill stipulating that there should never be an interval of more than three years between sessions. It moved on to declare ship money illegal and to attack the very existence of the Star Chamber and other tribunals. It then proceeded to the impeachment of Sir Thomas Wentworth, Earl of Strafford and Charles's Lord Lieutenant of Ireland, for high treason. The Lords acquiesced and Strafford having delivered up his sword, left the Chamber, 'no man capping to him before whom that morning the greatest in England would have stood uncovered'. The Commons then drew up the Grand Remonstrance and in doing so paved the way for the most dramatic event ever to take place in the Chamber.

A view of the Royal Court.

53

Charles I's holograph instructions on the imprisonment of the five Members.

Charles should have realized that attempts to silence his Parliamentary critics were doomed, but with that curious and childish obstinacy which was one of the more unfortunate hallmarks of his character he refused to heed the lessons of previous outbursts and, in January, 1642, urged on by his wife, marched the two hundred yards down Whitehall to arrest five Members who had caused him most annoyance, Pym, Hampden, Hazelrig, Holles and Strode. By the time he reached the Palace Yard the Members had gone. Unaware of this Charles advanced through Westminster Hall and sent word to the Speaker that he was present.

Fortunately for us, Rushworth, Clerk to the House, soon afterwards wrote a very detailed account of what happened. When he entered the House Charles uncovered, as did the Members. He approached the Chair and said to the Speaker, Lenthall, 'By your leave, Mr Speaker, I must borrow your Chair a little'. He then addressed the Members: 'Gentlemen, I am sorry of this occasion of coming to you. Yesterday I sent a Serjeant of Arms upon a very important occasion to apprehend some that by my command were accused of high treason; whereunto I did expect obedience and not a message. And I must declare unto you here, that albeit no King that ever was in England shall be more careful of your privileges to maintain them to the uppermost than I shall be; yet you must know that in cases of treason, no person has a privilege and therefore I am come to know if any of those persons who were accused are here.' Seeing they were not, he remarked, 'Well since I see all my birds are flown I do expect that you shall send them to me as soon as they return hither.'

He tried to discover their whereabouts by asking the Speaker. Lenthall, though bowing his knee in token of respect, replied in some of the most famous and significant words ever uttered in the Chamber; 'I have neither eyes to see nor tongue to speak in this place, but as this House is pleased to direct me, whose servant I am here; and I humbly beg Your Majesty's pardon that I cannot give any other answer than this to what Your Majesty is pleased to demand of me.' Defeated in his endeavours the King walked out, cries of 'Privilege,

Privilege' breaking out on every side of the House as he did so.

The result of this extraordinary episode was a total breach between King and Parliament. Within a matter of months the Civil War had begun. Lenthall's words, however, had a much more lasting effect. From that day no reigning monarch has ever entered the Chamber of the House of Commons, nor has there been any successful royal attempt to stifle the privileges of Members.

Not that Members were secure under the 'new order'. While the Civil War was raging, events at Westminster were not of such crucial account but with the ending of the war the issue was which faction of the victors should control the House, the Presbyterians or the Independents. The Presbyterians were able to summon the majority but this did not suit the purpose of the Parliamentary Army, and their most famous exercise of martial influence exceeded even the King's high-handed actions. Taking a large force from Hounslow, where the army was encamped, Colonel Pride stationed himself in the Lobby outside the Chamber and as the Members of whom he disapproved went by, and there were one hundred and fifty of them, he had them arrested. After 'Pride's Purge', as it became known, all that was left of the famous Parliament was a mere 'rump'. It was a Commons totally subservient to the army and the army was determined on one course of action above all others, the disposal of the King.

Charles I with his secretary, Sir Edward Walker, by an unknown artist.

Even before that black January day in 1649 when Charles was beheaded outside his own Banqueting House in Whitehall, the monarchy had been virtually abolished. The Great Seal of England, issued in 1648, substitutes for the monarch a representation of the Commons in session with the motto 'In the first years of freedom by God's blessing restored, 1648'.

This seal is one of the most accurate of the early representations of the Commons at work. All the Members are wearing their hats, and there are benches round and behind Mr Speaker's chair. The only inaccuracy is in the number: there are rather more Members than Colonel Pride had left behind. It was, however, important to elevate the position of the Commons for within a week of the death of the King the Commons was Parliament. A resolution was passed declaring 'The House of Peers in Parliament is useless, dangerous and ought to be abolished'. The Lords gone, there followed the ritual denunciation and official abolition of the monarchy. It was 'unnecessary, burdensome and dangerous to the liberty, safety and the public interest of the people of the nation.'

Charles II on his way to open Parliament.

The new strong man of British politics found even a relatively submissive Parliament as difficult and distasteful as his petulant predecessor had found a rebellious one, and in April, 1653, came Cromwell's famous dissolution. Going down to the House, again accompanied by an armed escort, he slipped into his usual seat in the Chamber and, when the Speaker rose to put the question, he addressed the House 'with the vilest reproaches, charging them not to have a heart to do anything for the public good, to have espoused the corrupt interest of Presbytery ... accusing them of intentions to perpetuate themselves in power had they not been forced to the passing of this Act (the Act of Dissolution) which he affirmed they designed never to observe; and thereupon told them that the Lord had done with them, and had chosen other instruments for the carrying on of His work that were more worthy'. This vitriolic speech provoked Sir Peter Wentworth to defiance. 'This was the first time he had ever heard such unbecoming language given to the Parliament, and it was the more horrid because it came from their servant, and their servant whom they had so highly trusted and obliged.' This was enough for Cromwell. Taking the floor of the House and saying, 'I will put an end to your prating,' he shouted, 'You are no Parliament; I say that you are no Parliament; I will put an end to the sitting. Call them in! Call them in!' Again soldiers entered and the Members of the Rump were driven out whilst Cromwell, turning to the table and taking up the Mace uttered his most quoted Parliamentary words, 'What shall we do with this bauble? Here, take it away.'

The doors were locked and the next day a notice appeared on them, 'This House to be let, now unfurnished.'

But even Cromwell found it difficult to exercise authority without an assembly to which he could refer and less than three months later a group, which has become known as 'the Little Parliament' (or, because of the strange assumed names of one of its more zealous Members, 'the Praise God Barebones Parliament') came into being. This fanatical assembly, which busied itself issuing decrees to 'level' property, religion and the law, quickly became embarrassing to its creator and when it turned its attention to the army Cromwell had had enough. In December, 1653, Parliament surrendered its power into the hands of a man who four days later was installed in Westminster Hall as Lord Protector.

The Lord Protector needed a Parliament too and in 1654 one was summoned to Westminster on his auspicious day—the day of all his great victories and of his birth (and death)—September 3rd. However, any hopes of its effectiveness were soon frustrated and within five months he had dissolved it.

The Parliament that was summoned the next year was not merely subservient, it was totally servile. It begged Cromwell to accept the crown. This he did not do, although he certainly assumed all the

trappings of monarchy and created a House of Peers in which, as Macaulay wrote, 'lucky draymen and shoemakers were seated, to which few of the old nobles were invited, and from which almost all of those old nobles who were invited turned disdainfully away'. Even the House of Commons, though it recognized him as Protector and would gladly have made him King, obstinately refused to acknowledge his new Lords. And so once again Parliament was dissolved, with the words 'God be judge between you and me'.

From then until his death in 1658 and the succession of his inadequate son 'Tumble-down Dick' as Lord Protector, Cromwell ruled without reference to any Westminster assembly. Richard Cromwell's rule was brief and inglorious and on 26 December the Rump of the old 'Long Parliament' was called together again. Lenthall, who had spoken those fateful words to Charles I, was again in the Chair but few of those who had given it distinction remained. It did, however, play something of a part in the arrangement which followed upon General Monk's declaration for a free Parliament. By its own Act it ceased to be on 15 April, 1660, a bare month before Charles II landed at Dover, 'to come into his own again'.

The 'Free Parliament' elected under General Monk's protection in the spring of 1660 was a constitutional anomaly. The King did not summon it: it summoned the King. It therefore became known as the Convention Parliament and on the arrival of Charles II at Dover its work was done. With its dissolution the twenty most turbulent years in the history of the Palace came to an end.

Though nothing would ever be able to erase the constitutional significance of those years, for the time being the Parliamentary pendulum had swung, and swung with a vengeance. The Convention Parliament underlined its loyalty to the new régime, if not its legitimacy, by ordering that the bodies of Cromwell, so recently 'the chief of men' and buried in great state, of Bradshaw, presiding Judge at the trial of Charles I, and of Ireton, Cromwell's powerful son-in-law, be disinterred and dragged on sledges to Tyburn. There they were hanged until sunset and then buried at the gallows foot. Later Cromwell's head was impaled on a spike above Westminster Hall where it remained for more than twenty years until it was dislodged in a storm and fell at the feet of a terrified guard.

The first elected Parliament of Charles II's reign was composed of Members 'of loyal families, but young men for the most part; which being told the King, he replied, that was no great fault for he would keep them until they got beards'. Charles was as good as his word: knowing that he would never again have such a Parliament, he kept them for eighteen years.

The Cavalier Parliament, as it came to be known, sat from 1660 until early in 1679, during which period it developed a relationship with the shrewdest of English Kings, which was to form the basis of our modern constitutional monarchy and to do more than anything to guarantee that the eighteenth century in Britain would be an age of

The cellars of the House of Lords where Guy Fawkes was discovered, as they were in 1807.

political stability. The Parliamentarians of Charles II's reign, like their predecessors in his father's, thus made their contribution, though in a different sense, to the preservation and enhancement of liberties which became the envy of continental Europe and in search of which continental Europe was plunged into upheavals which made our Great Rebellion seem like a series of mere skirmishes.

Relations between King and Parliament were not always smooth or easy. For all his political sensitivity—and he more than any other King understood that politics was the art of the possible—Charles did not take kindly to challenge or questioning, as Sir John Coventry, the Member for Weymouth, could have testified. In 1670 he made a critical reference to Charles's relations with actresses and was waylaid and savagely beaten. Though the act was denounced there was little doubt that the assault was instigated by the King. Coventry's was something of an isolated voice in 1670 but by the end of its life this once venal Parliament had become a real thorn in the King's side. He was increasingly jealous of its hold over supply, and it was increasingly suspicious, and not without reason, of the King's foreign policy.

Charles was a fairly frequent attender in the Lords during the early days of the Cavalier Parliament. He said he found the debates as good as a play, and he should have known. According to the historian, Bishop Burnet, he contributed to the informal theatrical atmosphere himself. When he first began to attend he would sit on the throne but, ever a restless man, he later took to standing by the fire, so attracting a crowd of admirers and rather disrupting the proceedings. This was not the only way in which Charles demonstrated a cavalier disregard of the dignity of the Cavalier Parliament in its early days. Pepys recalls

a celebrated incident in July, 1667, when the King had peremptorily summoned Parliament. It was the most difficult time of the year for many of the Members, bound up as they were with the concerns of agriculture. When they arrived at Westminster the first thing he did was to adjourn them for four days and then, as Pepys tells us, 'he did dismiss them to look after their own occasions until October'.

Members had thought he was going to consult them on the peace with the Dutch but he wanted them to know who was Master and told them, 'he had made a peace which he did believe that they would find reasonable, and a good peace, but did give them none of the particulars thereof. Thus, they are dismissed again to their general great distaste (I believe the greatest that Parliament ever was) to see themselves so fooled, the nation in a certain condition of ruin, while the King, they see, is only governed by his lust and women and rogues about him.'

In 1679 the Members were older and wiser and less easily deceived. The Parliament that had been elected in a frenzy of loyalty had, through a series of struggles with the King, acquired a real control over his accounts and was demanding an ever greater voice in his selection of Ministers and in his foreign policy. The number of veterans whom it contained still made it a 'safer Parliament' for the King than any possible alternative, however, and from 1676 he was constantly resisting demands for the dissolution of what its critics called 'the Pensioner Parliament'. When he did dissolve it in January, 1679, it was to save his Chief Minister, Danby, from almost certain impeachment. For the last session of Parliament from 21 October until 30 December, 1678, was a traumatic one. In September the infamous Titus Oates had testified before the Privy Council about the alleged 'Popish Plot'. This seventeenth-century McCarthy laid about him with vitriolic fervour that convinced many but did not deceive the King. Then two extraordinary events occurred which appeared to give credence to his tales. It was discovered that the Duke of York's secretary, Coleman, had been in correspondence with the Papal Nuncio and the French King's Confessor. And then Sir Edmund Berry Godfrey, the magistrate before whom Oates had appeared, was found murdered in a ditch.

When Parliament met, panic had seized the capital and those who were to be called 'Whigs' were in complete command of an ugly situation. No one dare oppose them for fear of having himself branded as a 'secret papist' and so the most disreputable resolution that has ever been presented to Parliament passed without a division in either house: 'There has been, and still is, a damnable and hellish plot contrived and carried on by Popish recusants for the assassinating and murdering of the King, and for subverting the Government and routing out and destroying the Protestant religion.'

Charles knew there was no truth in it but had little alternative when presented with Addresses by Commons and Lords, to sanction the enforcing of the most rigorous penal laws; to fortify Whitehall,

The Chamber of the House of Commons in the 18th century.

and to order all Catholic recusants ten miles from London. In Parliament itself guards were placed in the cellars where Guy Fawkes had stored his explosives and an Act was passed excluding Catholics from both Houses. This, however, was the end of unanimity, for now there was a real debate between Tory and Whig about whether the Duke of York should, in the light of the incriminating nature of the Coleman correspondence, be excluded from the succession. The Tories spoke of reverence due to royalty, the Whigs of the dangers to the Protestant religion.

This was indeed the time that the two political labels first came to be commonly used. As with so much that has passed into common and acceptable currency 'Whig' and 'Tory' were originally terms of abuse. The first Whigs had been, to quote Macaulay, 'persecuted Covenanters who had lately murdered the Primate (of Scotland)', whilst the first Tories were those 'Popish outlaws' who had taken cover in the Irish bogs to escape capture.

Now the terms were hurled across the Chamber in fierce debates over whether James's legitimate rights should prevail or Parliament should attach more importance to the risks of our having a Catholic monarch. The Whig view did not prevail but before Parliament was dissolved, Danby, the King's Chief Minister, had fallen, betrayed in effect by Charles. Danby had opposed the secret treaty which Charles had negotiated with Louis XIV in March of 1678, but to retain office he had swallowed his objections and his pride. Now Danby's part in the transactions (but not his reluctant acquiescence in them) was 'leaked' to the Whigs and the instructions, that Danby had written at his master's command, and on which Charles had scrawled, 'I approve of this letter, C.R.' was read to an astonished House of Commons.

That the King was deeply involved was allowed to pass. He, after all, was the intended victim of a far more sinister Popish Plot, and so the Whigs determined to impeach Danby. Had Parliament sat another month his head would surely have rolled, and so he persuaded the King, as a last act of gratitude, to dissolve the Cavalier Parliament.

Danby did more than survive. After five years in the Tower he came back into general favour and later held some of the highest offices of state, having come to terms with the Whigs, under William III. He was created a Marquis, and then a Duke (of Leeds) and, having survived another attempted impeachment, lived on almost to the end of Anne's reign.

The Whig Parliament that succeeded the Cavalier one was something of a Westminster 'witch hunt' and constant attempts, in an extraordinary atmosphere of suspicion and intrigue, were made to exclude James. Three exclusion Bills were presented in succession, and at one stage the King was obliged to exile both his brother James, and his bastard son, Monmouth, the Protestant claimant.

The third exclusion Bill was passed not in Westminster but in Oxford where the third Whig (or Oxford) Parliament of the reign met in 1681. Charles showed particular shrewdness in summoning it to this most loyal of cities for the Whig Members were deprived of the noisy support of the London mob. The King was determined to scotch any exclusion schemes. On the eighth day of the session he suddenly appeared in the House of Lords. He had been brought there in a sedan chair, followed by another with drawn curtains. When the Commons was summoned to the Upper House they expected to hear that the King had at last accepted their exclusion demands. Instead they found a composed and charming Charles, dressed in his robes of state, which had been secreted in the second sedan chair, in which alone he could dissolve Parliament. He did, and the Whigs went into oblivion until William III summoned his Convention Parliament nine years later.

The intervening period covered the last of Charles's reign and the three stormy and fateful years of James II's reign.

James's attempts to rule as a Catholic monarch failed lamentably. He had all the folly and none of the guile of his father and grandfather. He quickly alienated a Parliament which had initially been determined to be fair, though firm, in its relationship with him. Within three years he had thrown his seal into the Thames and gone into exile. This was taken as an abdication and William, Dutch Protestant husband of his daughter Mary, was invited to assume the throne with his Consort. It was essentially a Parliamentary invitation and so it was inevitable that the Whigs would dominate the Convention Parliament summoned to ratify the Orange succession.

James's folly had certainly damaged the Crown's standing. Now there could be no vestigial appeal to divine right. The King was there because Parliament willed it and, by the Declaration of Right and the Bill of Rights which followed, the tenure of the Crown was made strictly conditional. As the great historian Trevelyan says, 'All the outstanding disputes between King and subjects were decided against the King before the new monarchs were invested with their shorn authority. By this beneficent revolution the liberty of the subject and the power of Parliament were finally secured against the power of the Crown.' The new balance was never to be seriously disturbed.

Parliament's position and authority in the constitution were thus firmly set. Though the Monarch's influence was real, and at times even paramount, (as in the actual choice of Ministers), debates at Westminster took on a new significance where real decisions could be made—decisions that could not easily be overturned by royal whim or fancy. The establishment of Parliament's domestic supremacy was materially assisted by the fact that from 1689, when a Dutchman assumed the throne, until 1760, when George II died, we had, for all but the twelve years of Queen Anne's reign, a foreign-born sovereign whose interests lay primarily in the field of foreign policy.

It was appropriate therefore that it was during Anne's reign that the greatest constitutional change of the century—the Union of Scotland and England—took place. The crowns had been worn by the same head since James VI of Scotland travelled south on the death of

George II opening Parliament in the House of Lords, 1742.

of the GREAT SEAL.

KING sitting on his Throne, the COMMONS attending him at the end of y Session 1742.

...e, Baron Hardwicke, ...in the County of Gloucester, Lord High Chancellor of Great Britain

...est humbly Dedicated by his Lordships ...most oblig'd and most obedient humble Servant John Pine Bluemantle

Queen Elizabeth in 1603, but for over a hundred years after Scotland had its own Parliament. Now it was merged with England's.

The eighteenth century, like the seventeenth century, was very much a Parliamentary age, but in a different sense. The seventeenth century was the age of constitutional conflict and Parliamentary emergence: in the eighteenth century the authority of the Lords and (especially) of the Commons was firmly enough established for it to be the age of Parliamentary occasions and Parliamentary oratory.

Much of our present day precedent and procedure dates from those years. Parliament's place in the scheme of things being secure, Members could devote time and intellect to securing its proper operation. The most notable and continuing feature of eighteenth century Parliaments was the growing ascendancy of the House of Commons. Many of the leading statesmen of the time sat in the Upper House. Many of those who aspired to the Lower did so because they saw it as the ladder to noble preferment. But increasingly it was what was said and done in the Commons, the elected Chamber, that mattered. When Walpole, ennobled on his fall, met his old rival Pulteney (then Earl of Bath) he is reputed to have said, 'You and I, my Lord, are now two as insignificant men as any in England.'

Most of the great speeches of the century were delivered in the Commons and the tradition of brilliant, witty and often very lengthy Parliamentary oratory was established. Unfortunately we have no comprehensive verbatim reports of debates but those extracts and anecdotes which have come down to use are sufficient to confirm the tradition and frustrate the historian.

Sir Robert Walpole, who stood for the pocket borough of Castle Rising in 1701, and who later represented King's Lynn for most of the next forty years, dominated the Commons in the first half of the century. For twenty-one of those years he was, in all but name, Prime Minister. It was under his shrewd and skilful administration, which owed its longevity to his ability to handle men and anticipate crises, that the foundations of our system of Cabinet Government were laid.

Walpole was the first politician who fully realized the necessity of commanding a majority in the House. When he ceased to do so, defeated in a procedural vote on the Chippenham Election Petition—itself a culmination of a series of increasingly hostile votes—he resigned. In doing so he established an important principle—that a Minister who has lost the support of the House of Commons cannot continue in office. It is fitting that he should have fallen on a vote on a Parliamentary matter rather than a defeat on a major policy issue. For Walpole was, before all else, a great House of Commons man. He was the first Chief Minister who looked to the Commons rather than to the Other House for his main support and as his own proper place: 'I have lived long enough in this world, Sir,' he said in one of the debates on the war with Spain, 'to know that the safety of a Minister lies in his having the approbation of this House. Former Ministers, Sir, neglected this and therefore they fell; I have always made it my first study to

Robert Walpole and Speaker Onslow, c. 1740.

64

obtain it, and therefore I hope to stand.'

Walpole's great Parliamentary rival was that William Pulteney whom he greeted as the Earl of Bath. Their rivalry ranks with that of Pitt and Fox, and of Disraeli and Gladstone, in later Parliaments. Of the two Pulteney was perhaps the more accomplished debater. The Speaker for most of that period was Speaker Onslow, who said of him, 'He had the most popular parts for public speaking that I ever knew . . . he was as classical and eloquent in the speeches he did not prepare as the classical orators were in the most studied composition; mingling wit and pleasantry, and the application of even little stories, so properly to effect his hearers that he would overset the best argumentation in the world, and win people over to his side, often against their own convictions, by making ridiculous the truths they were influenced by before, and making some men afraid and ashamed of being thought within the meaning of some bitter expression of his, or within the laugh that generally went through the town at any memorable stroke of his wit.'

It was during one of the great Walpole/Pulteney debates that one of our least attractive Parliamentary traditions began — that of bringing in the sick to swell the numbers in the voting lobbies. One such group of invalids, we are told, 'had been placed in an apartment . . . their adversaries, aware of the fact, filled the keyhole of the door with dirt and sand which prevented their admission into the House until the Division was over. On this occasion, as General Churchill was sitting next to the Prince of Wales who was in the House of Commons to hear the debate, a Member was brought in who had lost the use of his limbs. 'So', said the Prince, 'I see you bring in the lame, the halt and the blind.' 'Yes', replied the General, 'the lame on our side and the blind on yours.'

In 1705 Governor Pitt of Madras wrote from Fort St George to his son Robert: 'If you are in Parliament show yourself on all occasions a good Englishman, and a faithful servant to your country. If you aspire to fame in the House you must make yourself a master of its precedents and orders. Avoid faction, and never enter the House prepossessed; but attend diligently to the debate and vote according to your conscience and not for any sinister end whatever. I had rather see any child of mine want than see him get his bread by voting in the House of Commons.'

No one could have taken a grand-parental injunction to heart more than Robert's son, William Pitt, who entered Parliament for Old Sarum, the rottenest of rotten boroughs, in 1735. Pitt did not take long to attract Walpole's attention, and apprehension. 'We must muzzle the terrible cornet of horse,' he said when he first heard his remarkable oratory. But 'the terrible cornet of horse' was irrepressible. He had great hopes and ideals untainted by financial ambition. He was not a rich young man but he was determined to do what he thought was right. His first seven years in Parliament were spent remorselessly attacking both Walpole and the King because he thought their measures either un-English, a subordination of English interests to Hanoverian, or a surrender to foreign arrogance and impudence. Walpole attempted to muzzle him by depriving him of his Commission, and thus of an income. This merely confirmed him in his determination, and made him something of a hero among his fellows. When he first attained office he baffled his friends as well as his critics by declining to follow well-established custom and refusing to use the opportunity (he was briefly joint Vice-Treasurer of Ireland and then Paymaster-General) to line his own pockets. The only fruit of office he would accept was the legal salary.

Pitt was at his greatest, and his oratory perhaps at his finest, during the Seven Years War with France — the first truly global conflict. The war began badly for Britain and the King, much against his own will, felt obliged to send for Pitt. His speeches during the war, as well as his conduct of it, had a Churchillian ring. From the outset he took the people into his confidence. As he told the Lords on another occasion, 'I despised the little policy of concealments. You ought to know the whole of your situation.' Thus when Fort Ticonderoga fell in 1758 he at once 'laid the whole detail open to inspection of the people at large, and by doing so ensured that confidence which a contrary conduct would certainly have deprived him of.' So when 1759 came — the year of victories — Pitt achieved the popularity he deserved.

Pitt was indeed the first truly popular Westminster figure called to supreme power 'by the voice of the people, expressed not as represented in Parliament but in the fact that "the eyes of an afflicted, despairing nation were now lifted up to a private gentleman of slender fortune wanting the advantage of birth or title".' He transmitted his own sense of determination and destiny ('I know that I can save this country and no one else can'), to such a degree that when he was briefly dismissed from his first Ministry the solid middle class of Scotland, England and Ireland, having no better means of expressing their sentiments, 'rained gold boxes' upon him by giving him the Freedom of the City of London and of no less than eighteen other principal cities, 'as a token of support, transcending that of an unrepresentative Parliament'.

It is small wonder that, like his equally great son after him, he identified the chief source of Britain's domestic and American troubles as the corrupt and defective electoral system. Indeed he suggested reforms that would have gone a long way towards making Parliament more representative of the people half a century before the great Reform Bill of 1832. Although he went to the Lords as Earl of Chatham, he was always known as the Great Commoner.

But it was as Earl of Chatham that he made his last speech during that war against the American colonies which he had so strongly opposed. ('I rejoice that America has resisted. Three millions of people so dead to all the feeling of liberty as voluntarily to submit to be slaves would have been fit instruments to make slaves of all the rest.') He had come down to the Lords to speak out but 'was not like himself'. His

Speaker Onslow presiding over the Commons, 1742.

HOUSE of COMMONS

A.D.		A.R.
1490	Richard Empson Esq.r	7 H 7
1494	S.r Reginald Bray	11 H 7
1495	Robert Drury Esq.r	11 H 7
1496	Thomas Inglefield Esq.r	14 H 7
1503	Edmond Dudley Esq.r	19 H 7
1509	S.r Thomas Inglefield	1 H 8
1511	S.r Robert Sheffield	3 H 8
1514	S.r Thomas Nevill	6 H 8
1523	S.r Thomas More	14 & 15 H 8
1529	Thomas Audley	21 H 8
1536	Richard Rich	28 H 8
1539	S.r Nicholas Hare	31 H 8
1542	Thomas Moyle Esq.r	34 & 35 H 8
1547	S.r John Baker	1 E 6
1553	S.r James Dyer K.t	7 E 6
1553 c	John Pollard Esq.r	1 Mary
1554	Clement Higham Esq.r	1 & 2 P.M.
1555	John Pollard Esq.r	2 & 3 P.M.
1557	William Cordel Esq.r	4 & 5 P.M.
1558	S.r Thomas Gargrave	1 Eliz.
1562	Thomas Williams Esq.r	5. Eliz.
1565	Richard Onslow Esq.r	8 Eliz.
1570	Christopher Wray Esq.r	13. Eliz.
1572	Robert Bell Esq.r	14 Eliz.
1581	John Popham Esq.r	23 Eliz.
1585	M.r Serjeant Puckering	27 Eliz.
1588 d	M.r Serjeant Snag	31 Eliz.
1593	Edward Coke Esq.r	35 Eliz.
1597	M.r Serjeant Yelverton	39 Eliz.
1601	John Crook Esq.r	43 Eliz.
1603	S.r Edward Phelps	1. Ja 1
1614	S.r Ranulp Crew	12. Ja 1
1620	Serjeant Richardson	18. Ja 1
1623	S.r Thomas Crew	21. Ja 1
1625	S.r Thomas Crew	1 Ch 1
1625	S.r Heneage Finch	1 Ch 1
1627	S.r John Finch	3 Ch 1
1640	Serjeant Glanville	16 Ch 1
1640	William Lenthal Esq.r	16 Ch 1
1660	S.r Hardottle Grimston Bar.t	12. Ch 2
1661	S.r Edward Turner K.t	13. Ch 2
1671	S.r Job Charlton	23 Ch 2
1673	Edward Seymour Esq.r	25 Ch 2
1678	S.r Robert Sawyer	30. Ch 2
1678	Edward Seymour Esq.r	30. C.H 2
	Edward Seymour Esq.r	
1679	M.r Serjeant Gregory	31 Ch 2
1680	William Williams Esq.r	32 Ch 2
1681	William Williams Esq.r	32 Ch 2
1685	S.r John Trevor K.t	1. Jam 2
1687	Henry Poule Esq.r	3. Jam 2
1689	S.r John Trevor K.t	1 W. M.
1694	Paul Foley Esq.r	7 W. 3
1695	Paul Foley Esq.r	7 W. 3
1698	S.r Thomas Littleton K.t	10 W. 3
1700	Robert Harley Esq.r	12 W. 3
1701	Robert Harley Esq.r	13 W. 3
1702	Robert Harley Esq.r	1 Anne.
1704	John Smith Esq.r	4 Anne.
1705	John Smith Esq.r	6 Anne.
1708	S.r Richard Onslow Bar.t	7. Anne.
1710	William Bromley Esq.r	9 Anne.
1713	S.r Thomas Hanmer Bar.t	12 Anne.
1714	Spencer Compton Esq.r	1 Geo 1
1722	Spencer Compton Esq.r	1 Geo 1
1727	Arthur Onslow Esq.r	1 Geo 2
1734	Arthur Onslow Esq.r	8 Geo 2
1741	Arthur Onslow Esq.r	15 Geo 2
1747	Arthur Onslow Esq.r	21 Geo 2

c. 1553	Serjeant Brooks	1 Mary.
d. 1585	Serjeant Puckering	28 Eliz.

of the   HOUSE of COMMONS in the Session 174½.

...r Onslow Esq.r ...   Speaker of the House of Commons.

...humbly Dedicated by his Honour's ...   most oblig'd and most obedient humble Servant John Pine Bluemantle.

FESTINA LENTE

speech faltered, his sentences were broken and his mind not master of itself. His words were shreds of unconnected eloquence and flashes of the same fire which he, Prometheus-like, had stolen from Heaven and were then returning to the place from whence there were taken.' Whilst answering the Duke of Richmond, 'he fell back upon his seat and was to all appearances in the agonies of death.' Within five weeks he was dead.

The man who was generally held responsible for the disastrous conduct of the war against the colonies was Lord North. His was a courtesy title, (he was heir to the Earl of Guilford), and so he sat in the Commons. However politically inept, he was personally amiable. Nothing seemed to ruffle his good humour. He had a reputation for slumbering on the Treasury Bench no matter how heated the debate. It was a habit that he doubtless cultivated and it certainly annoyed his opponents. 'Even now in the midst of these perils the noble Lord is asleep,' declaimed one. 'I wish to God I was,' came the reply.

The eighteenth century House of Commons abounded in full-blooded characters. It was hardly surprising that everyone who wanted to make his mark in the world aspired there. 'You will be in the House of Commons as soon as you are of age, and you must first make a figure there if you are to make a figure in your country,' wrote Lord Chesterfield in one of his famous letters to his son in 1749. All ambitious youths focused their aspirations on the Chamber of St Stephen's. 'To be out of Parliament is to be out of the world,' wrote Admiral Rodney from the West Indies in 1780, 'and my heart is set on being in.'

Who went to Parliament at this time? What sort of men made up the pre-Reform Parliament? First of all there were those who were predestined to political life, 'the inevitable Parliament men': the eldest sons of politically active Peers who took possession of one of the family boroughs as soon as they came of age. For such young men membership of the House was a duty.

After the scions of the great houses came the country gentlemen who often controlled merely a single seat. But though they were very independent and generally indifferent to preferment they did not coalesce easily; they formed no opposition in the modern sense and even their attendance was irregular and intermittent. Chesterfield, writing to his friend Bub Donnington in 1741, pointed out how necessary it was to get the opposition to meet before Parliament assembled. 'I have been these seven years endeavouring to bring this about and have not yet been able; foxhunting, gardening, planting or indifference having always kept our people in the country, till the day before the very meeting of Parliament.' They could be roused, as by Pitt, but they were content to represent their constituencies and look after their local interests, and to pay their national duties as circumstances inclined or dictated.

This meant that those who aspired to office or advancement had a good chance of achieving it, and a seat in Parliament, because of what

Presentation of the Sheriffs at Westminster, c. 1800. When the Law Courts were at Westminster it was the custom of the Sheriffs to attend in State on 23 June to be sworn in.

it could lead to, was the target of many eighteenth century 'social climbers', some of whom had only one thought in entering the Lower House: to get to the Upper.

Those who craved a coronet were generally well endowed with this world's goods, but there were those who entered the House to be better endowed and to whom Governor Pitt's injunction would have been anathema. To have control of patronage, to be able to reward these people, was to have control of votes. It might sound remarkably venal, but, today, a Prime Minister has something like a hundred Ministerial offices at his disposal and it is not unknown for friends to be rewarded with life peerages or seats on the Boards of nationalized industries! Who are we to adopt a censorious tone when we talk of people like James Hewitt, Member from 1761 until 1766 (he was afterwards Justice of the King's Bench and Lord Chancellor of Ireland), for writing that he has 'nothing to ask of Government for himself' but 'begs leave to recommend his brother, Mr William Hewitt, for something at home or abroad that may carry some public mark of respect to himself and, therein, do him credit'?

Apart from those who sought pecuniary advantages for themselves or places for their relations, there were those who went to Parliament as a means of professional advancement. In the eighteenth century there were few leading soldiers or sailors who did not sit in the House. In 1742 there were forty-four serving army officers in the Commons, and in 1754 there were at least fifty, all classified as 'for' the Government. Sixty-four officers were elected in 1761 including all the best known Generals of the time: Ligonier, Granby, Sir John Mordaunt, Clive, Burgoyne, Howe and Cornwallis. As with the army so with the navy: in 1741, 'most of our flag officers are in the House of Commons'. Sir Lewis Namier analysed the list of Admirals for 1761 and found that no less than twenty of the thirty listed either were, or had been, in Parliament, or were to enter it within a few years. Of the rest one had attempted to get in and had been defeated, another was a Scottish Peer, and another a member of the Irish Parliament. Senior Civil Servants such as the secretaries to the various Departments were also frequently in the House.

All this sounds strange today but the one profession that has preserved its close association intact is the law. Then, as now, lawyers abounded on the benches. A place in the House was a sure way to legal advancement. For the legal preferments open to Members were more numerous than today. The Attorney and Solicitor General to the Queen, the Solicitor to the Treasury, the Councils to the Board of Trade, Admiralty and other Government Departments were generally Members. It was possible too to be Master of the Rolls or one of the eight Justices of Chester and Wales, or a Judge of the Admiralty, and still retain one's seat. Many of these legal promotions were in fact a reward for services rendered, or promised, in the lobbies.

The Generals and Admirals were not the only ones connected with the almost unceasing armed conflicts of the eighteenth century who found it convenient to have a seat in Parliament. The elder Pitt's refusal to use his office as Paymaster to enrich himself, or dispense favours to others, was unusual enough to provoke considerable criticism from certain colleagues, for the holders of offices like his were eagerly courted by clothing manufacturers, corn merchants, ironmasters and timber dealers anxious for the numerous Government orders generated by the war.

Many of the merchants and bankers sat in Parliament, often encouraged to do so by the Government because they alone could afford to stand for those constituencies whose large electorates made it impossible for all but the wealthy to contest. During the course of the century almost all the great financial names were, at one time or another, entered on the Rolls of Parliament, and it was not thought at all untoward that there should be some direct financial advantage gained as a result of sitting in Westminster in order to support the Government of the day.

These were, then, the men who made up the eighteenth century House of Commons, augmented from time to time by those who sought a seat as a medieval fugitive sought sanctuary, as a means of immunity from the rigours of the law. Parliamentary privilege meant something in those days. The nabob returning from India who feared the way in which he had acquired his wealth might be subject to scrutiny, or the soldier who thought that his conduct in military operations might place him in jeopardy, knew that to be a Member of Parliament was to protect him from much, if not all, investigation.

It was a House of Commons composed of this cross section—the idealistic, the ambitious, the venal, the great and the insignificant, which a visitor observed towards the end of the eighteenth century when he wrote, 'I now, for the first time, saw the whole of the British nation assembled in its representative, in a rather mean little building that not a little resembled a chapel. The Speaker, an elderly man dressed in an enormous wig with two knotted curls behind, and a hat on his head, sat opposite me in a lofty chair. The Members had nothing in particular in their dress. They even come into the House in their greatcoats and boots and spurs. It is not at all uncommon to see a Member stretched out on one of the benches while others are debating. Some crack nuts, others eat oranges or whatever else is in season. Two shorthand writers sat not far from me and endeavoured to take down the words of the speakers; and thus all that is very remarkable may generally be read in print the next day.'

As the eighteenth century wore on there were increasingly remarkable events to report such as the debates and the uproar surrounding the repeated elections and expulsions of John Wilkes, that extraordinary rabble rouser and affluent debaucher whose name improbably became synonymous with liberty.

Wilkes, however, pales into Parliamentary insignificance beside four quite outstanding young men who rose to prominence during the last quarter of the century: Burke, Fox, Sheridan and the younger

Pitt, great-grandson of the Governor and son of the Great Commoner.

They were all great orators, though Burke, whose speeches have had the greatest influence since, made the least impression upon those country gentlemen and merchants who constituted the bulk of the Members of his day. Today his speeches are counted both as great literature, and, with the exception of his misconceived and immoderate harangues in Westminster Hall during the trial of Warren Hastings, remarkable contributions to political philosophy, but he was not always given a good hearing. On one occasion when he was being howled down he remarked that he could teach a pack of hounds to whelp with equal melody and equal comprehension. Another time he was very disconcerted by a Member who said, 'I hope the Hon Gentleman does not mean to read that large bundle of papers, and bore us with a long speech into the bargain,' and fled the Chamber. Of one of Burke's speeches however, delivered with great vehemence on the subject of the treatment of Indians during the American War, a diarist remarked that he was glad that strangers were excluded, because if they had been admitted the speech would have excited them to tear the Ministers to pieces as they went home.

Burke held office only briefly and his and Wilberforce's were the most distinguished backbench careers in Parliament history. Certainly no Members have had greater influence both in their own time and afterwards.

It was Burke who gave the celebrated definition, perhaps quoted more than any other by Members of Parliament since, of a Member as the representative of his constituents and not their delegate. He had a noble conception of Parliament and the roles and responsibilities of its Members at times of great crisis. As he said during a debate at the height of the war against the American Colonies, 'Magnanimity in politics is not seldom the truest wisdom and a great Empire and little minds go ill together.'

Among those who deserve to rank with him are Sheridan and Fox. Richard Brindsley Sheridan who entered Parliament for Stafford in 1780 was one of the most versatile of men. A notable dramatist, he became one of the greatest actors on the Westminster stage. A consummate master of Parliamentary oratory and repartee, his maiden speech was a disaster. 'I do not think this is your line' he was told, 'you had much better to have stuck to your former pursuits.' The rejoinder was typical, 'It is in me, however, and by God it shall come out.' Come out it did and he quickly established a reputation as the wittiest speaker in Parliamentary memory.

Fox was no mean judge of Parliamentary oratory and he was no mean performer. He took his seat at the age of nineteen as Member for Midhurst in Sussex, and before he was twenty he was on his way to establishing a reputation which few Parliamentarians at sixty could emulate.

Fox's drinking, his gaming and indeed everything about him was larger than life, but despite all the attractions of a dissolute life,

Charles James Fox, statesman and orator (1749–1806).

Parliament commanded his allegiance and affection, and before he had been in the House a decade he was acknowledged to be unrivalled in debate.

He was at his best when stretched, and stretched he was after 1781 when young William Pitt came into the House. There is an interesting story of how Fox's mother, Lady Holland, having just paid a visit to Lady Hester Pitt in 1767, wrote that very day to her husband describing the young William, then only eight years old, as the cleverest child she had ever seen. 'Mark my words, that little boy will be a thorn in Charles's side as long as he lives.'

At that time the young prodigy was often put on the dining room table to entertain his great father's guests. The training had its effect. Pitt's first speech was delivered with a 'fluency, precision and a dignity and a method which are usually the acquirement of many years of practice'. Lord North said it was the best maiden speech he had ever heard.

Burke, Sheridan and Fox made their reputations in opposition, Pitt quickly made his in office. In an age when it is considered remarkable to be a Cabinet Minister at forty it is almost impossible to conceive a young man of twenty-two being Chancellor of the Exchequer and a year later going from Number 11 to Number 10, Downing street as Prime Minister. And yet this is what Pitt did; from then (1783) until his early death in 1806 he dominated the House of Commons and British politics, leading his country both in peace and war. Out of office his influence was so great that a rhyme was coined when Addington, formerly Speaker, briefly assumed the Premiership:

> Pitt is to Addington
> As London is to Paddington.

With the deaths of Fox and Pitt in 1806 a golden era of Parliamentary oratory came to an end. The most commanding figure in the period immediately following was George Canning, but his career was sharply interrupted as a result of an altercation which he had with Castlereagh which led to their fighting a duel on Putney Heath. They were eventually reconciled and, after Castlereagh committed suicide in 1822, Canning became Foreign Secretary again.

William Pitt, the Younger, addressing the Commons, 1793, by Thomas Rowlandson.

It was in this second period of his holding office that Canning made one of the most significant pronouncements on foreign policy ever made in the Chamber. It not only spelled out British policy, it was in a very real sense the foundation of the celebrated Monroe doctrine. 'If France occupied Spain was it necessary, to avoid the consequences of that occupation, that we should occupy Cadiz? No, I looked the other way. I sought materials of compensation in another hemisphere. Contemplating Spain, such as our ancestors made her, I resolved that if France had Spain it should not be Spain with the Indies. I called the new world into existence to redress the balance of the old.' That speech, and a second that he delivered the same evening to reply to the debate, had a profound effect. One Member noted in his diary: 'It

was an epoch in a man's life to have heard him . . . Heavens! He
surpassed even himself. The chaste elegance, the graceful simplicity,
the harmonious tones of his opening speech, and the sublime energy
of his reply will haunt me to my grave . . . It was as if every man in the
House had been electrified. Tierney, who had been shifting in his seat
and taking large and frequent pinches of snuff, and turning from side
to side till, I suppose, he wore his breeches through, seemed petrified
and sat fixed and staring with his mouth open for half a minute.
Canning seemed actually to have increased in stature, his attitude
was so majestic.'

Brougham, who was not too well disposed towards Canning,
acknowledged that he displayed 'a degree of fervour unprecedented in

the effect even beyond the Rt Hon Gentleman's former most eloquent orations.' Brougham himself was the other great debater of this pre-Reform era, a man able to hold the attention of the House for six hours on one occasion and, who despite a prickly temper, had a great popular following, a following considerably enhanced by his eloquent upholding of the pleas of the undeservedly popular Queen Caroline at the time of her trial in the House of Lords in 1822.

This trial was one of the three most notable events to take place in the Old Palace in the nineteenth century. Accused, and with good grounds, of adultery by the new and unpopular King George IV, she was hailed as something of a heroine. Brougham, chosen as her Attorney General and charged with the duty of defending her, championed her cause with a fervour that was echoed by the cheering crowds that waited upon her public appearances and surrounded the Houses of Parliament throughout her trial. So great was the official apprehension that soldiers were posted in rooms and lobbies around the House of Lords Chamber where her trial was held, and her progress from St James's Square, where she was lodging, to Westminster was a triumphal one. To the people she was a wronged and courageous woman, pursued by Ministers who had suppressed the liberties of the nation. Even Wilberforce wrote, 'One cannot help admiring her spirit but I fear she has been very profligate.' The popular agitation lasted throughout the extraordinary trial, from mid-August until early November when the Bill to dissolve the King's marriage and to deprive the Queen of her title was passed by a mere nine votes. The Lords had obviously found her guilty but questioned the expediency of the measure. Sensing there was little chance of passing it through the Commons the Government dropped it. At this news the whole of London was illuminated and the Queen's popularity reached its zenith. It soon waned, however, for in January she accepted an offer of £50,000 a year and a residence and, no longer a symbol of resistance and oppression, but just another 'pensioner' she ceased to be a popular champion. She featured briefly on the Westminster stage the following summer when she sought admission to her husband's Coronation, but the doorkeeper of the Abbey would not let her in and when she gave up the attempt the crowd, momentarily on her side again, turned against her. Within a month she was dead.

Of the other two great Parliamentary occasions that must be referred to one was brief and tragic, the other laid the foundation for a new era. The brief and tragic one was the assassination of Spencer Perceval. He was an unremarkable Prime Minister but a good man whose most memorable achievement was the making of bank notes legal tender. He was shot in the Members' Lobby on 11 May, 1812, by a deranged bankrupt called John Bellingham who had a grievance against the Government. Walpole had once been severely set upon in Westminster Hall but in all the upheavals of the seventeenth and eighteenth centuries no violence of this sort had ever occurred within Parliament, and despite the activities of the Fenians and others, Perceval's death remained the only occasion when a leading British politician had been assassinated within the precincts of the Palace until the brutal murder of Airey Neave in March, 1979.

The event which marked the opening of a new era was the last great Parliamentary occasion in the Chamber in which the Commons had sat for close on three hundred years: the passing of the great Reform Bill. The crucial vote, when the House took the fundamental decision on Parliamentary reform, was on the Second Reading of the first Bill on 21 March, 1831. The best picture we have of the occasion comes from the pen of Macaulay, himself Member for Leeds at the time and an ardent supporter of the Bill. It is, in fact, the most vivid eyewitness account we have of any Parliamentary occasion and comes from a letter he wrote to a friend just a few days afterwards.

'Such a scene as the division of last Tuesday I never saw, and never expect to see again. If I should live fifty years the impression will be as clear and as sharp in my mind as if it had just taken place. It was like seeing Caesar stabbed in the Senate House, or seeing Oliver taking the Mace from the table, a sight to be seen only once and never to be forgotten. The crowd overflowed the House in every part. When the strangers were cleared out and the doors locked we had six hundred and eight Members present, more by fifty-five than

The Trial of Queen Caroline in the House of Lords, 1820.

The assassination of Spencer Perceval, 1812.

were ever in a division before. The Ayes and the Noes were like two volleys of cannon from opposite sides of a battlefield. When the Opposition went into the Lobby, an operation that took twenty minutes or more, we spread ourselves over the benches on both sides of the House; for there were many of us who were not able to find a seat during the evening. Everybody was despondent. "We have lost it. We are only two hundred and eighty at the most. I do not think we are two hundred and fifty. They are three hundred. Alderman Thompson has counted them. He says they are two hundred and ninety-nine." This was the talk on our benches . . . I had no hope, however, of three hundred. As the Tellers passed along our lowest row on the left hand side the interest was insupportable,—291, 292 . . . we were all standing up and stretching forward, telling with the Tellers. At three hundred there was a short cry of joy, at three hundred and two another, suppressed, however, in a moment, for we did not know what the hostile force might be. We knew, however, that we could not be severely beaten. The doors were thrown open and in they came. Each brought a different report of their numbers . . . We were all breathless when Charles Wood, who stood near the door, jumped on a bench and cried out, "They are only three hundred and one". We set up a shout that you might have heard at Charing Cross, waving our hats, stamping on the floor and clapping our hands. The Tellers scarcely got through the crowd, for the House was thronged up to the table, and all the floor was fluctuating with heads like the pit of a theatre. But you might have heard a pin drop as Duncannon read the numbers. Then again the shouts broke out and many of us shed tears. I could scarcely refrain. And the jaw of Peel fell; and the face of Twiss was as the face of a damned soul; and Herries looked like Judas taking his necktie off for the last operation. We shook hands and clapped each other on the back, and went out laughing and crying and huzzaing into the Lobby. And no sooner were the doors open than another shout answered within that House. All the passages and stairs into the Waiting Rooms were thronged by people who had waited until four o'clock in the morning to know the issue. We passed through a narrow lane between two thick masses of them and all the way down they were shouting and waving their hats, until we got into the open air. I called a cabriolet and the first thing the driver asked was, "Is the Bill carried?" "Yes, by one vote". "Thank God for it Sir!" And away I rode to Gray's Inn and so ended a scene which will probably never be equalled until the reformed Parliament wants reform.'

The days of the old un-reformed Parliament were numbered. Though that Bill foundered, within a year a similar Bill was on the Statute Book. But the new Parliament was not destined to meet in the old Chamber, scene of so many stirring events, for much longer. Less than two years after it met for the first time St Stephen's Chapel was in ruins.

The passing of the Reform Act in the House of Lords, 1832—note the empty benches on the Conservative side of the House.

CHAPTER THREE

The New Palace – Competition and Acrimony

No longer shall forsaken Thames
Lament his Commons House in flames.
A pile shall from its ashes rise
Fit to invade or prop the skies.

AMONG the many thousands who saw the Hall silhouetted against the sky on the night of 16 October, 1834, was Charles Barry, an established architect with a number of major public buildings to his credit. He was returning on the Brighton coach when he saw 'a red glare on the London side of the horizon' and discovered that the Houses of Parliament were on fire. He spent the rest of the night in the crowd 'absorbed in the terror and grandeur of the sight'.

He was not the only onlooker whose life was to be transformed by the blaze. Somewhere in the vast crowd was another and much younger man who had decided to devote his life to the study and practice of architecture. Augustus Welby Pugin was only twenty-two but was already an expert on Gothic architecture. Both men watched the conflagration with mixed feelings.

Pugin rejoiced at the miraculous saving of the Hall, though he grieved at the destruction of so much he admired, especially the Painted Chamber. But 'it was a glorious sight to see much of Soane's mixtures and Wyatt's heresies . . . effectually consigned to oblivion.'

He was filled with gloomy forebodings, however, speculating on the uninspiring and unimpressive edifice that he was sure would be erected in place of the lost Palace.

Barry too was depressed, but only by what he saw destroyed. His imagination was fired by the thought of the opportunity and challenge the task of replacement would bring to some ambitious architect.

These feelings were widely shared among those who lamented rather than cheered the destruction. There were, as we have seen, many who had long moaned the cramped conditions in which Parliament had operated, and agitated for their improvement, or indeed advocated the building of a new purpose-built parliament house. Now it could be built and the miserable and squalid conditions in which the nation's legislators had been obliged to operate become a memory of the past, while a fitting seat for the government of 'the mightiest nation on earth' was constructed.

The 'new Palace' school, however, were not to find their views universally accepted. Amid the destruction and the devastation some walls still stood and there were those who advocated restoration and repair as the only proper course which anyone who viewed Parliament with a sense of history or a thought for economy would contemplate.

There were prominent architects on the side of the restorers too. James Savage was one. His special thought was for St Stephen's Chapel, 'the walls of which even in their present state of dilapidation have a solidity that could not be surpassed and that probably could not be equalled by a modern building'. His appeal in the columns of the *Morning Herald* was pedestrian compared with the purple passage with which William Etty, a member of the Royal Academy and one of the most fashionable artists of the period, ended a lengthy letter published at the same time (March, 1835): 'I call upon you then, artists of Britain, as you value the noble country that gave you birth, as you value the divine arts you profess, as you value your own fame and reputation to protect these glorious remnants! To watch them with a jealous eye and guard them with a miser's care, resist their destroyers wherever and whoever they are as the enemies of your country and as the invaders of your natural and national inheritance. Believe me, the opportunity of saving them is not lost, no patchwork plagiarism from Greece or Rome can supply their place . . . They are existing and pleasant evidence of our greatness as a nation and of our former progress in those arts that embellish and add so many charms to existence; connected as they are so intimately with our history, forming so noble and beautiful a feature in our ancient national character and shedding around our land as they yet do the halo of their sanctity and their glory.'

The reformed House of Commons: it had to make do with temporary accommodation for almost twenty years.

Some who were moved by these pleas and accepted the argument for restoration and recreation, nevertheless equally accepted that Parliament needed better and more commodious quarters, and there were many suggestions that it should move. Some wanted the King's offer of Buckingham Palace, newly completed at enormous cost, accepted. Others thought that somewhere in the region of St James's Park and adjacent to those clubs, 'to which most Members belong and the streets where most lived,' would be suitable. Their argument was that destruction had severed the ties that bound Parliament to Westminster. Restoration could provide suitable extra Government offices, but even razing to the ground would not provide an adequate site for the fine new parliament house that was needed.

These were minority views, however. That there should be a new building, that it should be at Westminster, and that it should incorporate the Great Hall was a view to which most Members of the first Reformed Parliament subscribed.

Those with radical leanings were not, however, the only ones who had cursed the inconvenience of the Old Palace. John Wilson Croker, who had resigned in disgust at the passing of the Reform Bill,

described the conditions in which Members of the House of Commons had to work as 'notoriously imperfect . . . They are not well disposed to the transaction of business; they are not symmetrical with the House of Lords; they are not symmetrical with Westminster Hall; there is no proper access for Members although we have the misfortune to see the Prime Minister murdered in the Lobby; and on several occasions Members have been personally insulted in going to the House. A Member who does his duty in Parliament is sometimes liable to offend individuals; he must pass every day of his life in a series of narrow, dark tortuous passages where any individual who wishes to insult him may have the certain and easy opportunity of doing so.'

Long before 1832 the increasing work of Parliament made the Palace totally unsuited to the effective, let alone comfortable, conduct of business. A mass of legislation is no new parliamentary phenomenon; in 1824 there were as many as forty-four Bills under consideration by Committees, sometimes on a single day, and the Committees had to meet in the most cramped, congested and inconvenient rooms imaginable.

Conditions in the Chamber itself were notorious. There were frequently four or five hundred Members there and in the Lobby, and the staleness of the air was such that in 1831 a Select Committee had

been set up to see how St Stephen's could be made 'more commodious and less unwholesome'.

Before the turn of the century Sir John Soane, builder of the law courts adjacent to Westminster Hall, had produced plans for two houses of neo-classical design (St Stephen's was to be restored for public worship) in response to requests from the Lords. However, the financial strain of the Napoleonic Wars effectively aborted any scheme to build new Chambers.

The Committee of 1831, chaired by Sir Frederick William Trench, did not come up with any coherent plan, and so the first Reformed Parliament established another Select Committee, this time under the radical Joseph Hume. Thirteen architects gave evidence, including Soane. He stated quite frankly that 'It was totally impossible by any means whatsoever to enlarge the House of Commons sufficiently'. Only one of the architects, Hopper, suggested that the old House could be sufficiently and properly altered. A whole series of designs were suggested for the new Commons Chamber, circular, semi-circular, oblong. Some wanted an octagonal chamber like a Cathedral Chapter House 'where it was necessary that each Member should deliver his sentiments from his place, sure of being heard equally well by all present'. In one thing most concurred: there must be room for the Press. As Hopper said, 'I know how anxious the constituents are to know what their representatives are doing, and as the reporters are the champions of conveying that information, it seems to me desirable that they should have the best means afforded to them.'

The fire ended all arguments about adequacy but the immediate problem was to provide accommodation for the Members for the session that was about to begin. Few took kindly to the thought of meeting away from Westminster and so Robert Smirke, architect of the British Museum and of the new Covent Garden Theatre and, with Soane and Nash, one of the three men appointed as architects to the Board of Works, was summoned by the Prime Minister and the First Commissioner of Woods and Works. He reported that the walls of the House of Lords were strong enough for it to be fitted as a temporary Commons and designed a temporary home for the Lords in the ruins of the medieval Painted Chamber. He made a good enough job of the operation for the cost-conscious *Morning Chronicle* to comment at the beginning of the 1835 session, 'We do not conceive that there will be any necessity to erect a new building.' This was a view that was certainly not shared by the Earl of Wicklow whom *Hansard* for 12 March 1835 reports as demanding that 'something be done for the accommodation of their Lordships with respect to the present House of Lords during the period of the building of the new one, for in the dog days they would find it almost insupportable.' The Marquess of Westmeath agreed, remarking that 'under the galleries they were almost smothered'.

A different style of Chamber: the Irish Parliament in 1780—abolished by the Act of Union of 1801.

As early as November, 1835, Lord Melbourne's First Commissioner of Woods and Works, that same John Cam Hobhouse who had done so much to salvage the records during the fire, had asked Smirke to prepare plans for rebuilding the Houses of Parliament on a 'moderate and suitable scale of magnitude.' Later that month there was a change of administration and Peel became Prime Minister for a few months. However, the rebuilding was not the first of his concerns and he allowed Smirke to produce designs that would then be submitted to Committees of both Houses.

This was just what Pugin had feared: 'I am afraid the rebuilding will be made a complete job of, as that execrable designer Smirke has already been giving his opinions, which may be reasonably supposed to be a prelude to his selling his diabolical plans and detestable details. If so I can contain myself no longer but boldly to the attack will write a few remarks on his past work and if he does not writhe under the lash his feelings must be harder than cement, as, if I spare him, I hope to sink myself. His career has gone on too long and this will be a capital opportunity to show up some of his infamous performances.'

Pugin was especially vitriolic but few today would deny that most of

Smirke's work, however competent, was dull, pedestrian, run of the mill neo-classical stuff, and when rumours began to circulate that he was indeed to be entrusted with what Barry later called, with some justice, 'the largest and most elaborate architectural work ever perhaps undertaken at one time in this or any other country,' there was considerable murmuring, reinforced both by criticism of a number of recent public works and also by the knowledge that the main contract for work on the temporary houses had gone to Smirke's brother-in-law.

The fundamental criticism was, however, not one of impropriety. Smirke's character in these matters was reckoned to be beyond reproach. The serious criticism was generated by lack of confidence inspired by his lack of genius. This was not, so the argument went, a matter for MPs to decide on their own, a contract they could privately award. The capital city must have a Parliament building that truly reflected Britain's and London's position in the world. The 'mother of Parliaments' must be 'worthy of being the Palace of the constitution which its authors boast of having effected so great an improvement of the Old English government.' Here was 'an opportunity of redeeming the age from the obloquy to which it had become exposed, from the gaudy attire and ephemeral character of its metropolitan offices, and erecting at least one structure worthy of being placed beside the noble monuments of St Petersburg and Paris.'

Sentiments like these merely echoed what so many had been saying from the moment the fire subsided. *The Spectator*, for instance, just a week after the event, had held forth, 'The Palace of the legislature, where the laws are propounded and settled, and the interests of a whole people are discussed, should include every accommodation that past experience, and forethought of the prospect of future improvement, may show to be required. It is a structure to endure for ages ; and as such should anticipate as far as may be foreseen future wants . . . The cost is not an object ; money is not to be wasted but it is not to be spared.' It was up to the two Houses to determine the accommodation that they needed and that in turn should determine the site, and then the design itself should be obtained by a competition open to all 'foreign as well as native artists'.

This call for a competiton was rapidly taken up. As *The Westminster Review* urged, 'Let the House pass resolutions as to the general nature of the objects to be accomplished and afterwards cause the plan to be the subject of a competition by all the skill the country can supply.' *The Times* joined in and Sir Edward Cust, a veteran of the Peninsular War and a Member of Parliament from 1818 until the passing of the Reform Act, wrote an open letter to the Prime Minister in which he recommended the setting up of a Commission of 'gentlemen interested in architecture' whose task it would be to organize and judge a competition for designs for the new Houses of Parliament.

The Commons did in fact set up a Committee, early in 1835, to consider the whole question of rebuilding but initially only Joseph

Two rejected designs: above by C. R. Cockerell, who based his design on Greenwich; below by David Mocatta.

Hume, Chairman of the former Select Committee, was convinced that open competition was the best means of discovering the best architect and design. His colleagues seemed perfectly happy to accept Smirke's scheme. They felt increasingly isolated in their satisfaction, however, and quite quickly, bowing to the pressure of opinion as expressed in both radical and Tory journals, committees in the Commons and the Lords decided that they would indeed have a competition and appoint a Commission to oversee it.

The Commission was duly appointed and the rules of the competiton laid down. Appropriately, Sir Edward Cust was one of the Commissioners, the others being the Hon Thomas Liddell, son of the Earl of Ravensworth, an enthusiastic supporter of the Gothic and something of an amateur architect himself, George Vivian, who had written several pamphlets on architectural improvements in London, including one on 'The Prospects of Art in a future Parliament House,' and finally a Member of Parliament, Charles Hanbury-Tracy. He was an amateur architect of considerable distinction having designed his own great house at Toddington, in Gloucestershire, in the Gothic manner. Being the only Member of Parliament he acted as Chairman of the Commission. The banker and poet, Samuel Rogers, was also invited to join but he declined, as did Lord Aberdeen and Lord de Grey, the first President of the Institute of British Architects. All of the Commissioners were amateurs because it was thought that if professional architects were appointed they might well be influenced by professional jealousy.

The Commissioners' terms of reference were very strictly defined. Anyone would be free to enter the competition but only so long as he submitted a design in Gothic or Elizabethan style. He was to conceal his identity by motto or pseudonym, and between three and five prizes of £500 each were to be awarded for the selected designs. The winner would be given a further £1,000 if he did not secure the appointment to superintend the building. All entries were to be submitted at the scale of twenty feet to an inch and to be executed in Indian ink. No coloured drawings were to be allowed in case they misleadingly influenced the amateur judges, but the competitors could submit three sepia-tinted perspectives taken from points specified on the lithographic plan with which they were supplied on payment of one pound, which acted, in effect, as an entrance fee. Competitors were also to be sent a copy of the resolutions of the rebuilding committee and the evidence that had been presented to it.

There was general satisfaction with the rules, the noted architect C. R. Cockerell describing the competition as 'a model in most respects.' However, there was criticism of the decision to limit entries to the Gothic or Elizabethan styles. Much more was to be heard of this later. Even at the outset, although there was fairly general agreement that a Gothic Palace might well be suitable in view of its proximity to the Abbey and because of the agreed need to incorporate Westminster Hall. Few people seemed to know quite what was meant by

'Elizabethan style'. Pugin commented rather contemptuously on the 'fashionable rage for this architecture—if it can so be called'. However, those who drew up the rules were obviously influenced by the kind of arguments which had been deployed in *The Quarterly Review* in 1831, which praised the Elizabethan as being an exclusively *English* style. 'There is something in the rich irregularity of the Elizabethan architecture, its imposing dignity, gorgeous magnificence and quaint and occasional fantastic decoration reminding us of the immortal bard of the same age.' It was doubtless these romantic associations with the Virgin Queen and her court, and with Shakespeare and the other great figures of that age, which made it seem, to those who drew up the rules, an ideal architectural vehicle for the great new Palace of a new great age.

Be that as it may there was considerable agitation that classical architecture had been excluded. There was criticism too, though in a much lower key, of the choice of Commissioners. J .C. Buckler, who would obviously be among the competitors, had worked closely with Hanbury-Tracy whilst Barry had been associated with Cust. These, however, were minor quibbles. Apart from the stylistic objections the only real quarrel was over the time allowed: three months. Nevertheless, it was the same for all and the competition excited considerable professional interest, an interest that was to be confirmed by the remarkable number of entries.

Barry's original design—later modified.

The principal reason why competitors objected to the three months rule was that the specifications to which they had to work were very exacting. The site was an awkward rectangle, some eight hundred feet by three hundred and fifty, but it had to include Westminster Hall and take account of other 'geographical' restraints. The Abbey, Bridge Street, and St Margaret's were all considerably inhibiting factors, not to mention the river. As for the building itself it had to provide the sort of accommodation which Members were used to in the grand and splendid Clubs, like the Athenaeum, and Barry's Travellers' which were springing up in and around Pall Mall.

The Lords' Chamber 'should be capable of containing three hundred Peers, allowing two foot for each, and the breadth should allow one more row of benches on each side than in the old House.' There had to be a Lobby and separate galleries for MPs and strangers, and also two others. There must be a Royal Robing Room, six Committee rooms and six waiting rooms, rooms for Peers' servants, coffee rooms and dining rooms and kitchens, a vote office and rooms for, among others, the Lord Chancellor (five) the Earl Marshal and the Bishops. Residences for the Black Rod, the Principal Doorkeeper and the Housekeeper were specified, as was a detached guard house for three officers and a hundred men.

The specifications for the Commons were even more demanding. There had to be sitting room for between 430 and 460 Members in the body of the House and adequate accommodation for all the rest in the galleries. There must be a large Lobby adjoining, as well as voting lobbies, galleries, thirty Committee rooms, two dining rooms, rooms for the Clerk and his assistants, the Clerk of fees and Clerk of Journals, etc, etc. There must be an especially splendid house for the Speaker, the first Member.

Remembering the problems caused in the old House it was not surprising that the Commissioners demanded 'special provisions for ventilation' of all rooms. Perhaps the feature which most distinguished the proposed new Palace from the inadequate old one was the insistence on adequate library provision. It was not until 1818 that a room had been set aside for a Commons Library, and then it had been a small and cramped one. Now there were to be three rooms, all of them sixty by twenty-eight feet, as well as apartments for the Librarian. The Lobbies, too, were to be extensive. They had to be in the new age when all Members had constituents to serve and sometimes to see. Gone were the days of the pocket and the rotten boroughs where a Member

could represent a mere handful of electors.

Competitors were also asked to bear in mind the needs of particular rooms. Libraries and committee rooms had to be quiet and the committee rooms easy of access for witnesses. The refreshment facilities must be close to the Chambers. Notwithstanding the allure of the prize money—£500 for three months' work was reckoned princely ('the most munificent I ever heard of one competitor called it), and the national, and indeed international, prestige that would attach to the winner, the competition was so complex and the odds against winning so high that not every leading architect felt that he could risk three months' total involvement.

Very many did, however. According to the catalogue of designs exhibited later at the Royal Academy there were ninety-seven entries, not counting that of Francis Goodwin who died before completing his. Among the prominent architects who entered were C. R. Cockerell, Gillespie Graham, Thomas Hopper, Anthony Salvin (one of Nash's favourite pupils), and James Savage who had written that spirited letter to the *Morning Herald.*

Although most of the designs are now lost, enough survive to give us an idea of the vast range of treatment and of talent. Some, like Savage, were concerned to create an imposing building 'with a definite purpose and not an aggregate of different buildings grouped together by accident'. Others, like Gillespie Graham, thought that was just the way not to do it and the interest would be heightened by diversity. Hopper set out to treat 'the entire mass of buildings . . . as a single edifice.' Donaldson, who had started work in a merchant's office in the Cape of Good Hope and was later to become Professor of Architecture at University College, London, chose to compose in distinct units and varied styles so that he 'could avoid a series of the same effects'. Lewis Cottingham, a prolific restorer of churches, had the same concept, but he put it rather splendidly. It was his aim, he said, to avoid 'the all roundalike monotony of the ditto repeated'. There were those who wanted a castellated effect, and yet others who went for the 'rich and cloistered'. Pembrose Pointer, architect of schools and churches and one of the founder members of the Royal Institute of British Architects, was one of many who experienced acute difficulty in accommodating the great Westminster Hall with its enormous roof, 'the vomitory of the law courts' he called it. Others felt they must retain St Stephen's Chapel and, if possible, the other adjoining medieval buildings. As Adam Lee put it, 'This glorious edifice of the third Edward must be restored'. And yet if it were, what should be done with it? It was, after all, too small for the new House of Commons to be accommodated in anything like comfort.

During those three hectic months in 1835 these were some of the problems which exercised the minds of the competitors. None, however, was so great as that presented by the enormous river frontage which the site allowed to be anything up to a thousand feet in length. No one in this country had any experience of giving a

Sir Charles Barry by J. P. Knight.

'monumental character' to a facade approaching so great a length. To cope with this particular problem a variety of devices were applied. One entry made a special feature of a magnificent Speaker's House. Cockerell, who was later to design the Taylorian Building at Oxford, the Fitzwilliam at Cambridge and St George's in Liverpool, unashamedly based his design on the royal Palace at Greenwich. Some, like George Harrison and J. T. Knowles, went in for towers and spires.

As for style, most of the entrants chose the Gothic option, although one of the younger architects, David Rhind, who chose as his motto '*pro patria semper*', did try his hand at the Elizabethan and received an accolade from *The Gentleman's Magazine*. His design, they thought, was *the* outstanding one, 'decidely magnificent, the style pure, the ornaments well selected and admirably arranged, the different constituent features finely proportioned and harmonized'.

When it came to the Gothic most of the great existing examples were ecclesiastic and this was reflected in the entries. *The Architectural Magazine* judged most of the designs too ecclesiastical or 'at best too monastic'. *The Morning Chronicle* thought a number represented 'the elongated side of a cathedral with transept, and interspersed to vary the line.' The magazine stigmatized Hopper's efforts in particular as being 'a congregation of English cathedrals'.

The competitors were not all architects. William Wilkins, architect of St George's Hospital and the National Gallery, complained bitterly that 'carpenters, bricklayers, house agents, artisans and even amateurs submit their plans with the same confidence as the proved and experienced architect'. One of them, William Buckland, admitted that he had never received any instruction in drawing or design.

From this medley of the competent, the ingenious, the bizarre and the plain ludicrious, the judges had to pick five winners. Because of the protests over the time limit, competitors were, in fact, given a month's extension until the first of December, 1835, and the judges found their task so difficult that they in turn asked for an extension until the end of January before announcing their verdicts. The ninety-seven entries involved consideration of almost fourteen hundred drawings.

From those entries they selected not five but four designs and by unanimous agreement first prize went to Charles Barry. 'Although difference of opinion may exist between the ground plans separately considered, we are all unanimous in our opinion that the one delivered to us numbered 64, with the emblem of the portcullis (Barry's hallmark) bears throughout such evident marks of genius and superiority of talent as fully to entitle it to the preference we have given it . . . And we have no hesitation in giving it as our opinion that the elevations are of an order so superior, and display so much taste and knowledge of Gothic architecture as to leave no doubt whatever in our minds of the author's ability to carry into effect Your Majesty's commands.'

The other prize winners were J. C. Buckler, David Hamilton from Scotland and William Railton, who later designed the Nelson memorial in Trafalgar Square. Little attention, however, was paid to their efforts, one writer to *The Times* even going so far as to suggest that they had merely been selected as foils to Barry's masterpiece. This was less than fair as all three architects did submit plans of considerable ingenuity, any one of which, had it been finally selected, would have led to the erection of a notable building.

However, there could be no doubt that Barry deservedly won the palm. He incorporated features common to many of the entries but handled them with a subtlety and delicacy which was the work of a sure master. The immediate reaction to his success must have pleased the judges. *The Gentleman's Magazine* spoke of their soundness of judgement, whilst *The Times* said that Barry's design, 'was undoubtedly splendid . . . One of the completest as a whole and one of the most artistlike and scientific in design and arrangement.' *The Athenaeum Magazine* was even more fulsome. Barry, it said, 'had entered into the spirit of our national style and made an original and palatial elevation.' The approbation was not universal, however, *The Morning Herald* launched and maintained a positively vindictive campaign designed to have the judges' verdict overturned and Barry's design rejected. 'The four worthy Commissioners,' it thundered, 'may rest assured that towards them personally we cannot be guilty of any disrespect as we believe them to be very gentlemanly in their manners; but we do certainly dispute the infallibility of their judgement, and still more do we maintain they are not sufficiently well informed either in the theory or in the canons of good taste in architecture, and are not at all acquainted with its practical operations . . . Though pretty to the uninformed eye it (Barry's design) is meretricious . . . The chaste and truly beautiful St Stephen's Chapel is completely sacrificed.' *The Herald* was especially severe on Barry's plan to move 'the noble south window of Westminster Hall forty feet further to the south . . . As for the House of Commons, it has the most extraordinary gallery we ever saw connected with a senate house and very much resembles one of the shilling galleries in one of our great theatres.' It went on to allege that since the award Barry had been allowed to alter his plans significantly and 'the alterations will increase the expense by £50,000 . . . In fact it is no longer the contrivance to which the amateur architects gave the first prize. These gentlemen have proved how little capability they possessed for the work which they vainly usurped, and we are sure that the nation and justice demand that competent judges and a proper adjudication should now be granted to the country.'

The Herald was commenting on the public exhibition of all the submitted designs held at the National Gallery. It saw the exhibition as an opportunity to persuade both Commons and Lords to think again. Others, like Brayley and Britton, in their Preface to *The Ancient Palace and Houses of Parliament, Westminster* gave a rather less biased view

Back benches in the Lords showing the ornate carving.

and merely welcomed the fact that the exhibition was being held. 'An opportunity will thus be afforded for the public to examine and compare the various and numerous designs which have been made for this important mass of public edifices . . . We hail the event and the epoch as of incalculable importance to the profession, to the public, and to the national character. We are sanguine enough to expect that it will be the first of an annual exhibition of architectural models, drawings, casts and engravings by which the artists will be able to display their respective powers and qualifications. The nobility and gentry will be better instructed in the arts of architectural composition and the public mind be much improved in all matters connected with this most important branch of the fine arts.'

The exhibition had, in fact, been staged because of requests following a meeting of competitors held almost immediately after the judges' Report was issued. The meeting, chaired by Peter Robinson, himself both a competitor and Vice President of the recently formed Institute of British Architects (he had entered under the optimistic pseudonym '*dum spiro spero*'), whilst welcoming the competiton as 'beneficial to the artists of the country', and praising the judges' ability and impartiality, petitioned Parliament to provide for a full exhibition of all the plans, 'to allay any apprehensions in the public mind with respect to the propriety of the decision'.

Pamphlets poured forth and the parliamentary air was rent with all manner of accusations. Joseph Hume even divided the House in an attempt to have the whole affair reconsidered. The vulnerability of the amateur judges was revealed when he asked Hanbury-Tracy, the Chairman of the Committee, about such things as ventilation, acoustics, light and the durability of the ornamentations of Barry's design. He alleged that the small courts behind the river front would be ill-ventilated and that they would make the surrounding rooms stuffy and dingy.

Cross-questioning revealed that the Commissioners had, in fact, encouraged the prize-winners to revise their designs. This, of course, was grist to *The Herald*'s mill and the basis for its accusations of substantial redrawing. In a series of articles on the exhibition *The Herald* pressed home the attack, asserting that 'all the foreground plans (of the winning entry) were in bad arrangement and very deficient in the extent of the accommodation required'.

There were, it claimed, 'six or seven sets of drawings in this exhibition equal, if not superior, in general appearance to that of Mr Barry but much superior in true taste and scientific practicability'. One of the designs which was 'correct and in good taste' and 'like many which we have noticed in our remarks very superior in all those points to the designs which have so strangely been passed upon the Parliament as deserving the prizes which were intended for merit only' was submitted by William Wilkins. Wilkins certainly seems to have adopted the maxim 'in defeat, defiance'. Infuriated by his failure in a competition which he had in the first place fiercely opposed, he attacked Cust as the charlatan who misrepresented the truth and was merely out to reward Barry for services rendered—at public expense. This outburst provoked Savage to turn his wrath upon Wilkins' own rather insipid and indifferent design. 'His unsupported assertions will not be accepted as truths that the servile copying of details and parts of classical buildings will compose a building which will emulate those of ancient Greece.' The old controversy over the styles themselves was thus revived. Why had there not been an opportunity for 'the style of the times' to be deployed?

The controversy rumbled on, and occasionally erupted, all through the first half of 1836 and indeed beyond. William Richard Hamilton, the antiquary (not to be confused with the David Hamilton who had carried off one of the four prizes), was particularly and elegantly critical in a series of letters which he addressed to the Earl of Elgin, Chairman of the Trustees of the British Museum and the man responsible for appropriating the celebrated marbles. He wrote to 'one who has done more to enrich your country with splendid productions of Grecian sculpture and Grecian architecture', to deplore the fact that no regard had been paid to the classical. 'It is . . . deeply to be regretted

Augustus Welby Pugin.

The Prince's Chamber.

that on an occasion which was regarded by the whole of Europe as likely to lead to the construction of an edifice which, with the resources of the British Empire and the talents and ingenuity of British artists, might eclipse everything of the kind that Europe had yet seen . . . Gothic barbarism is again to be allowed to triumph over the masterpieces of Italy and Greece . . . Britons are, henceforth, to look for the model of what is sublime and beautiful in art to the age of ignorance and superstition.' He had more grounds than the purely aesthetic for taking this line. 'We are all sensible of the daily inconvenience from the increased consumption of coal in every part of the city and the injury done to the appearance of our public edifices where there are many projecting members with intricate details cannot have escaped notice . . . Now Greek architecture is of all others the best adapted for avoiding this crying nuisance . . . When William II built the Hall he did not prescribe that it should be constructed after the style in vogue during the dynasty of his Saxon predecessors . . . and when the same building was restored under Edward III and Richard II the style prevailing under those sovereigns, not that of three hundred years ago, was adopted.' He ended with a plea that 'we should indulge a hope that the legislators will pause in their proceedings before they come to a final decision.'

All was in vain. By the time Hamilton printed his letter the Commons had made its decision and so had the Lords, and neither House could be prevailed upon to reverse it.

Barry himself had been called before a joint meeting of the Lords and Commons to explain his design. He showed that he had, in fact, taken note of Joseph Hume's objections, widening the internal courts and extending the building towards Millbank. He had altered his two original towers and provided a clock tower. Hanbury-Tracy had, all along, made it plain that, 'Mr Barry may go on improving his plan and I trust that if it is adopted it will be improved from time to time until the building is completed.' Barry, however, realized the sort of charge that would be levelled at him if he appeared to have made too sweeping changes.

On 28 April, 1836, sixteen days after Barry's evidence, the Lords Committee, in its second and final report, recommended the adoption of Barry's plan, although it added a rider, 'considering the magnitude of the expense to be incurred such arrangements will,' it trusted, 'be made by Government as will secure the greatest vigilance and economy in carrying the object into effect, both with reference to the just remunerations of the persons to be employed and the details of the work itself'.

The Commons Committee held its final session on the next day and again the question of cost was high on the agenda. Barry took his Quantity Surveyor, and also Thomas Chaner, official Surveyor to the Office of Woods and Works. He explained that his estimate of £724,986 was based upon the work he had done at the King Edward VI School in Birmingham, taking into account the extra prices charged in London for labour and materials. On 9 May the Committee recommended to the House that Barry's plan be adopted for a sum, 'not exceeding by any considerable amount, the estimate submitted.' It would not however, 'be safe or expedient to engage in a work of such magnitude and importance until a due and accurate estimate, founded on detailed specifications and working drawings, should have been made and carefully examined and approved by competent authority.'

Barry was therefore enjoined to produce these drawings in time for the next session. He was to be paid a special fee for the purpose but there was no guarantee either of 'the ultimate adoption of the plan' or that he would be retained for superintending the execution.

While Parliament was taking what, in the event, turned out to be momentous decisions, the exhibition of the rejected designs was being held. The sub-committee of the exhibiting architects, headed by Cockerell, presented their petition to Parliament, asking that a Commission of Enquiry be set up before a final verdict. This is what prompted Hume's abortive Motion.

Nevertheless with the closing of the exhibition the carping and sniping and criticizing of the rejected candidates almost came to an end. A year later the Duke of Cumberland presented a Petition in the Lords on behalf of Lewis Cottingham which sought to demonstrate that the first prize was given for a design 'which did not comply with the particulars issued by the Office of Woods and Works' and begged their Lordships, 'to institute an enquiry into the truth of the allegations contained herein'. Viscount Duncannon, *Hansard* laconically records, 'said a few words in defence . . . of the conduct of the Commissioners and of the course they adopted.'

It was, in fact, generally accepted both in Parliament and outside that the Commissioners had, whether by good fortune or sound judgement, made the right decision. *The Morning Herald* spoke for very few and certainly today there can be almost no one who would deny that the right man was in the right place at the right time and that his presence was properly noticed. Whether it was suitably rewarded is another matter for though now the way was clear for Barry to proceed, it was a very rough and rugged path he had to tread. His New Palace of Westminster took more time and consumed more money in the building than ever he had bargained for, and its slow erection was punctuated by criticism and controversy, besides which the acrimony of the last few months would pale into significance.

Close-up of one of the carvings in the House of Lords.

CHAPTER FOUR

The House That Barry Built

The architect surveys his plan: the statue of Sir Charles Barry erected in his memory and situated on the staircase to the Committee corridor.

SMARTING after a long inquisitorial session in front of a Select Committee, Charles Barry wrote to his friend and collaborator, Pugin, 'I am in a towering rage and in the right humour for tearing up my appointment at the New Palace of Westminster, which I expect I shall be driven to do before long. All the arrangements for the new House of Commons, including the form, size, proportion, taste, and everything else concerning it are in abeyance and await the fiat of a Committee of the House of Commons, of all tribunals the most unfit to decide.'

The date was 1844. It was nine years since Barry had won the competition and over eight since he had told the Commissioners that he envisaged his masterpiece could be completed within six years and at a total cost of £800,000. It was seven years now since the first estimates had been passed by the Commons, and four since the foundation stone had been laid. All of these years had been marred by confusion and controversy. Still neither Commons nor Lords had a new Chamber in which to meet and the man whose designs had been approved and whose previous career had shown that he was capable of decisive execution of elaborate schemes was understandably frustrated and annoyed. The euphoria of 1835 had given way to considerable bitterness by 1844.

Perhaps more than anything else Barry resented what he reckoned was the ignorant and unwarranted interference with his professional duties, and the unnecessary challenging of his professional skills, by men whose origins might have been more exalted than his own but whose ability to judge and discern, and to supervise the creation of his great Palace, was manifestly inferior.

Barry was at once proud of his achievements and conscious of his humble origins. Perhaps an underlying feeling of social inferiority made him ill at ease in the company of those whose elegance and graces he may have envied but whose judgement he openly despised. All this meant that he frequently reacted with a truculence that did not endear him to those to whom he was technically responsible, but it is one of the sadder episodes of Westminster history that the building of the Palace was not a more enjoyable task for its architect, and that the man who gave Britain the greatest of its nineteenth century buildings was so little appreciated by those whom he strove to serve. This was a misfortune made all the greater in that Barry undoubtedly sacrificed innumerable other commissions, and no doubt smoother personal advancement, in dedicating himself for the last twenty-five years of his life to the New Palace.

Barry was not yet forty when he watched the old Palace burn, but already he had achieved notable success. He was born in Bridge Street, Westminster, on 23 May, 1795. His father was a stationer of modest means, most of his income derived from Government contracts. Charles had a difficult childhood. His mother died when he was three and his father when he was ten, losses for which even a devoted and affectionate step-mother could never compensate. His schooling was perfunctory and of the three establishments he attended, one at least was wholly inadequate. There, we are told, 'The master paid little attention being dissolute and absenting himself for weeks together.' When he left at the age of fifteen he took articles with a small firm of architects and surveyors in Lambeth. A love of buildings and a talent for drawing them had attracted him to the architectural profession and he very quickly made his mark, having his first drawing accepted at the Royal Academy's annual exhibition in 1812 when he was barely seventeen. It was an interior of Westminster Hall.

For the next few years he sought to master the techniques of his chosen profession but he firmly believed that there was no substitute for the close study of great buildings and in 1817 he decided, having first become engaged to Sarah Rowsall, another stationer's daughter, to spend a couple of years and his small legacy on a Grand Tour of the great architectural monuments of Europe and the Middle East. He was away for three years, sketching and noting all the time. He was able to extend his tour because he fell in with a Scotsman named David Baillie who was so taken by the young man's drawings that he agreed to take him on to Egypt and Syria, paying Barry £200 in return for a series of sketches, of which Barry was allowed to make copies.

He was the most perceptive of travellers, capable of appreciating the different beauties of Gothic and classic, equally fascinated by the cathedrals of France, and the temples of Baalbek. He was not afraid to risk arrest—as he did on two or three occasions—because of his insatiable inquisitiveness, nor to criticize even the best-regarded of buildings like Milan Cathedral where he found 'a want of harmony and continuity in its parts'.

In 1820 he returned and settled in a small house in Holborn. It was not easy for a young man of little means and with few influential connections to attract private commissions of note. But there was one way in which the young architect could seek public recognition, one way in which Barry could aspire to have his name bracketed with the great and recognized architects of the day, Nash and Smirke, Wyatt and Soane: the public competition.

This was an age of public building and frequently contracts were awarded following open competition. Barry began entering competitions almost as soon as he returned to London. Inevitably most of his early attempts were unsuccessful. He failed, for instance, to get the commission to build the Leeds Exchange, or the Law Society in London, or churches in Newington or Kensington or Streatham. He

The Commons Chamber as completed in 1852. Against his will, Barry had to make numerous modifications to this design.

was not deterred, even though to that list of 'failures' he had to add the Westminster and Charing Cross Hospitals.

His first break came in 1822 when his services were retained by the Church Commissioners for two new churches at Prestwich and Campfield in Manchester. Emboldened by this success he felt confident enough to marry Sarah.

Over the next few years he built up a well-regarded practice and by 1828 he was winning important competitions and commissions. His was the design selected for the Travellers' Club in Pall Mall. Later he was to be given the task of designing its neighbour, the Reform Club, and most reckon that, after the Palace, to be his greatest masterpiece. His services were retained in the provinces too, to build the City Art Gallery in Manchester and King Edward VI School in Birmingham.

His work demonstrated a remarkable versatility and showed that he had truly mastered what he had studied on the Grand Tour. The Clubs in Pall Mall were the most successful of Italianate nineteenth century buildings, while King Edward's was a masterpiece of what he called 'Tudor Gothic'.

It was an architect, therefore, of diverse accomplishment and wide experience who had been selected to execute the greatest commission since Wren had built St Paul's Cathedral after another great fire, but Barry was to find his parliamentary masters even more testing and tetchy than Wren found the Canons of St Paul's.

The building of the Palace as seen from Carlton House Terrace, by David Hall McKewan.

Complaints about the Commissioners' decisions having been finally dealt with, Barry's initial problems were not architectural ones. The site on which he had to build could not, in purely physical terms, have been less suited to a great building. River sites are never easy to build on and this one was particularly difficult because the ground was so swampy. His first task was to create a great coffer dam and then to sink enormous deep concrete foundations on which the vast pile could be erected. It was not until April, 1840, that the foundation stone for the new Palace could be laid. Already there was such a degree of scepticism and so many criticisms were being voiced about the project that it was no great royal or parliamentary personage who performed the quiet ceremony, but Mr Barry's wife. The choice was appropriate but the reasons for it were not calculated to fill the proud husband with confidence.

Well might Barry have watched with apprehension as the stone was laid, for the remaining twenty years of his life were to be among the most frustrating any artist can ever have faced in the execution of a masterpiece. A corporate patron is always the most difficult to satisfy and there had never been a more difficult corporate patron than the Victorian Lords and Commons.

One of Barry's major initial difficulties was caused by the reluctance of either House to leave its temporary quarters. The Lords were in the patched-up Painted Chamber and as the moment for the destruction of the hallowed ruins approached everything possible was done to cause delay. A reluctance to sever a tie of five centuries and to see the

last traces of one of the glories of medieval architecture razed to the ground was understandable but it was very frustrating for the architect. It was not until 1847 that Barry was finally able to pull down the Chamber.

He had even more trouble with the Commons, who were meeting in the old Court of Requests, formerly the Banqueting Hall of the Royal Palace and later the Court in which Petitions to the King were heard. It had been fitted up as a very acceptable temporary Chamber, the most attractive feature of which was an excellent system of ventilation installed by a Dr Reid. The approbation that he won for this was later to result in his being one of the sharpest thorns in Barry's side.

In the early years of the construction, however, Barry's main worry was a very basic one: finance. It was commonly accepted that an architect's commission was five per cent of the outlay of the work in question. But Parliament was the guardian of the public purse and public buildings were expensive undertakings. Nash had recently exceeded by nearly half a million pounds the £200,000 estimate he had calculated would be the cost of rebuilding Buckingham Palace. The nation's legislators were nervous lest a similar disaster overtake the estimates for their own Palace. What they did not appreciate was that they would be much more likely to save the public funds by giving an unfettered command to the architect and enabling him to make smooth and easy progress than if they questioned and thus delayed his every move.

Times were not propitious. The revenue was falling and in 1841 Peel had been obliged to reintroduce (as a temporary expedient) income tax—at seven (old) pence in the pound! Against this background, therefore, they felt no compunction in paying Barry a bare three per cent of his original estimate of £800,000—a commission of £25,000 on the whole building.

Whether the cost could ever have been held to this figure, however quickly progress had been made, is highly unlikely. Certainly Barry never had a chance to prove the accuracy of his original figures and he had to cope with political masters who took the superficially logical view that one of the best methods of keeping the cost down was, 'to pay the architect as little as possible, as infrequently as possible and with as much fuss as possible'.

While Barry was fighting for what he considered a just reward for his labours the masons on the river front were witholding theirs. For almost two years they were on strike. Their industrial inaction, following upon the first two years building, which was largely occupied with getting the foundations right, meant that there was never any chance of the whole edifice being completed before the very end of the 1840s.

Nevertheless, within a few months of the laying of the foundation stone there was a general acceptance that something of vast importance was happening on the banks of the Thames, that a very great building was in the course of construction. The new Prince Consort saw it and realized what a splendid setting it would be for great paintings and great sculptures. And so, under Prince Albert's efficiently benign Chairmanship, a Commission was appointed to superintend the embellishment of the building. It was a powerful Commission and included Lord Palmerston, Lord Melbourne, Peel and Lord John Russell, and, of course, the Speaker. Its only notable omissions were Barry and Pugin. Neither the architect nor his brilliant though eccentric collaborator, Augustus Welby Pugin, whose principal task was the internal adornment and enrichment of the Palace, 'in the best Gothic taste', were ever consulted about the appointment of the Commission. So it was that many of the statues erected and paintings commissioned, both in Barry's lifetime and afterwards, were somewhat out of sympathy with their setting. Mercifully Barry and Pugin, after being threatened that they would have the Committee's 'assistance', were left in charge of all the internal decorations of the building, other than paintings and sculptures. For that at least we must be thankful, but any visitor cannot help but notice the glaring difference in quality between Pugin's exquisite work and the frescoes in which some of the more exciting episodes in Britain's history are garishly depicted. What would Pugin or Barry have thought of that extraordinary picture in the Commons' corridor which shows Charles II being met at Dover in

The Lord Chancellor greets Black Rod in the Peers' Lobby, c. 1860.

1660 by a sycophantic reception Committee, one of whom carried a Union Jack?

But the wrangling over fees (and that continued throughout the progress of the work) and the unwelcome intrusion of the Commission were not the greatest of Barry's worries and frustrations. Rarely can an architect have had greater responsibility and less power. His was the conception, and his the duty of execution, but at every stage he was subject to supervision and interference, hauled before Select Committees to explain and expound and justify, and saddled with decisions in which he had had no part and the consequences of which were sometimes potentially catastrophic for his grand design.

Perhaps the greatest of all his problems was caused by the appointment, without reference to him, of that David Boswell Reid who had so effectively devised the scheme for the ventilation of the temporary Chamber in the Court of Requests. That achievement, and the doctor's constantly reiterated concern for the state of Members' health, so endeared him to the two Houses that he was retained to supervise the heating and ventilation of the Palace.

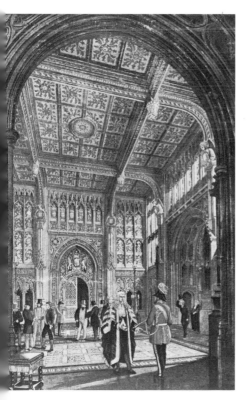

One has to sympathize with the Members to some degree. London was a foul and smelly place before the advent of modern sanitation. We have seen how, even before the destruction of the old Palace, there was continual concern and criticism of the 'noisome' Chamber. There may have been an odour of sanctity across the road in Westminster Abbey: very different aromas pervaded the air in the secular cathedral opposite. For hundreds of years people had associated pestilence with smells and the fact that Doctor Reid had created a tolerable atmosphere in the Court of Requests made it natural that he should be thought of as the one to make the great new Palace wholesomely habitable. There was a sharp reminder of the need for fresh indoor air during the summer of 1847 when the stench of untreated sewage in the Thames was said to be so bad that Members had to flee a Committee Room to escape the 'pestilential' odours.

Whatever his competence in small things, however, Doctor Reid was not technically qualified to cope with the enormous problems of ventilating a great Palace. His schemes were more remarkable for their vague generalities than for their detailed specifications, and for several years there was a constant battle between Barry and Reid in which the authorities frequently took the side of the engineer. When it looked as though almost a third of the building was to be taken up by ventilation cavities Barry became incensed, saying that to make any scheme such as Reid proposed work, 'great mechanical skill, a thorough knowledge of the art of construction, sound judgement and decision, and, in fact, the methods and habits of a man of business would be required, in all which attainments and qualities of mind, Dr Reid is, in my opinion, most certainly deficient.'

After five years of charge and countercharge the rival claims of Barry and Reid were finally, at the architect's request, submitted to arbitration. The independent expert brought in, Joseph Gwilt,

produced a report scathing in its comments of Reid's scheme and endorsing Barry's objections. Reid petitioned against the decision, but in 1846 his appointment was terminated by the Lords and shortly afterwards he left the Commons' service too.

For one thing all admirers of the Palace must be grateful to Dr Reid. It was because of his scheme's requirements that Barry had to incorporate the new and graceful tower and a number of other ventilating spires, not in his original design, which are such a picturesque features of the building, though one must add that the central tower has never been used for its intended purpose!

It is interesting to note that even in 1978 Members of Parliament were not very satisfied with the heating and ventilation of the building. In March of that year a Motion appeared on the Order Paper of the House of Commons, complaining about the intolerable heat in the basement and the intolerable cold on the top floor!

The dispute on ventilation was far from the only subject on which Barry found himself constantly questioned. When he wrote the letter quoted at the beginning of this chapter, he had just been giving extensive evidence to a Select Committee which was angered by the slow rate of progress of the building, and this in spite of the reluctance of the Lords and Commons to vacate their temporary accommodation. As one sympathetic questioner put it, one of Barry's major difficulties was 'the necessity of combining the actual sitting of the two Houses in something like their present locality with the progress of the work surrounding them'. But few questioners were sympathetic, especially in the Commons. Nor was Barry always tactful in his replies. A monosyllabic 'no' would frequently be all the answer he would volunteer to what he considered to be an unnecessary question. He did not suffer Parliamentary fools gladly.

By 1847, the Reid business having been largely disposed of, the emphasis was increasingly on cost. The original estimate had already been exceeded by £600,000—'a more profligate and gross expenditure of public money has never taken place'. Joseph Hume, who had done so much to try and defeat the Barry design, expressed the opinion that the architect 'should be put under curb and bridle for he has had his own way too long'.

One senses a certain smug satisfaction in Barry when one reads the answers he gave indicating that a great deal more money would still be needed before his masterpiece was complete. If the fools would delay the public would have to pay.

When the matter was debated in the House Sir Robert Peel joined forces with the Government who had defended Barry and the estimates, and said that the blame should not be attached to the Government but to the House itself, 'first for insisting in limitations of expense, and then for expressing dissatisfaction with the poor results obtained after required limits had been imposed'.

The towers over the South Wing and one of the ventilating shafts made necessary by Dr Reid's scheme.

In 1848 there was an attempt to free the architect from the restraints of a Select Committee. A Royal Commission was set up consisting of only three Members, Lord de Gray, and Thomas Greene MP, with Sir John Fox Burgoyne, Inspector General of Fortifications, as independent chairman. The Commission was charged with the task of superintending the completion of the New Palace, 'with reference to designs approved and the amount of estimates laid before Parliament'. It was also enjoined with the task of approving the 'decoration, furniture, clocks and bells' required to complete the Palace, and to decide upon all the arrangements for heating, lighting and ventilation. It was this Commission which received and approved Barry's estimate for a final completion figure of another million pounds in February, 1849. This became the occasion for another Parliamentary attack, an attack coupled with a dispute over decorations during which the Commons petulantly reduced the estimates by a token £1,000 to express their displeasure at the fact that Landseer had been paid that amount for some pictures in the Lords of which they disapproved. Caught between the Treasury and Parliament, the Royal Commission recommended its own dissolution.

It was small wonder that Barry was driven almost to distraction on occasions. He had two Ministerial overlords, the Office of Woods and

Works, to whom he was directly responsible, and the Treasury, which always lurked in the background and had much greater power than the minor Department. He had to satisfy the Commons and the Lords in the persons of their Select Committees. He had to cope briefly (the least of his problems) with the Royal Commission. In addition the Lord Great Chamberlain and the Speaker had to be consulted for the Palace was a royal one and the Speaker its most distinguished inhabitant. Almost daily for over twenty years Barry was summoned to explain himself or to justify his actions to some committee or individual.

Never did he come closer to despair than when the Commons rejected their new Chamber. In spite of the fact that they had been reluctant to move out of the Painted Chamber, the Lords did accept Barry's replacement with good grace when they occupied their new House for the first time in February, 1847. Some of the Peers found the acoustics difficult to get used to but they persevered and initial scepticism and minor criticism were soon replaced by general approbation and real pride.

The Commons reacted very differently when they first sat in their new Chamber three years later, in May, 1850. Complaints rained in on every side. In the beginning Barry had planned a Chamber capable of seating six hundred Members of Parliament with commodious public galleries. When the plans were discussed, however, he was prevailed upon to scale down the conception of the vast debating hall. This he did, and succeeded in creating a masterpiece fit to rank with his House of Lords at the other end of the corridor. The Members were not pleased. The ceilings were too high. They could not hear themselves speak. It was all most unsatisfactory. Barry was reduced to distraction by the Members' total inability to adapt to the new and elegant surroundings he had provided for them. They even had the gall to say that there was not enough room either for themselves or in the Strangers' galleries—in spite of the fact that Barry had had enormous difficulty in persuading the Building Committee that there should be any accommodation for women visitors at all.

And so the Commons adjourned in high dudgeon to the Court of Requests and did not re-enter their new Chamber until February, 1853. During their absence Barry busied himself with alterations with which he thoroughly disapproved and which, in his opinion, destroyed the scale and symmetry of his masterpiece. He had to instal a false ceiling with sloping sides and cut out the great and lovely windows. The new and distorted proportions made such a mockery of his original conception that he never again willingly entered the Chamber he had been obliged to vandalize. The Commons quickly took to it, however, and ever afterwards referred to it as 'Barry's Chamber'.

There was acrimony over the clock as well. It was not until the clock tower was a hundred and fifty feet high that a clock was commissioned from a Pall Mall clockmaker, Vulliamy, who was invited to submit a design. He did so only to find the Government had

The New Palace from Lambeth, c. 1850.

decided that the design of the clock should be the subject of a closed competition. In the end the contract went to Dent, largely, it was suspected, because the adjudicator, the Astronomer Royal, had claimed that Dent was the greatest living clockmaker. As it was the maker was dead before the clock was ready, completed by his son, in 1855. When it was installed the large bell, known as Big Ben after Sir Benjamin Hall,* the Commissioner of Works, cracked while it was being tested and had to be recast. It was hung again in 1850 and was again found to be cracked. The solution proposed was to substitute a lighter clapper and turn the uncracked surface towards it. This solution was finally adopted but Big Ben as we know it did not toll over Westminster until 1862, by which time Barry had been dead for two years.

*Although some say it was so named, by the workmen who moved it, after Benjamin Caunt, a famous prize fighter of the day.

He died in May, 1860, just before his sixty-fifth birthday and within a few hours of being at work on the finishing touches of his great Victoria Tower. This was his supreme architectural achievement. It was the highest tower in the United Kingdom and its weight was consequently enormous. The sheer technical accomplishment of building it on what was essentially a base of quicksand was itself remarkable, but the greatest triumph lay in the mastery of proportions which made it possibly the most beautiful single structure erected in the nineteenth century, and one of the loveliest towers in the world.

Though he was still working on it at his death it had been all but completed for eight years. In 1852 Queen Victoria had arrived for the State Opening of Parliament and driven under the Tower. Whether she was conscious of the great engineering feat (the erection of a cast iron skeleton) that had made its construction possible, her husband was. At any rate she was conscious of its beauty and proud that it bore her name. Shortly after that State Opening Barry was knighted.

His knighthood was one of the few happy episodes in the long and involved saga of the building of the Palace. Perhaps the unhappiest was the Pugin controversy which raged after Barry's death and cast a shadow over his achievement.

It was tragically ironic that the controversy should have arisen as a result of one of Barry's most notable qualities—his ability to select and delegate. He was determined from the outset that the Palace should be as beautiful and as dignified in its external details and in its internal decoration as in the 'grand design' and to this end he formed groups of craftsmen accomplished in stone and wood carving, in cabinet making and metal working, in glass and decorative painting, and even in encaustic tile making. As the Dictionary of National Biography has it, 'He was gifted with that intuitive knowledge of men who could be of use, which characterized the first Napoleon and which is possessed by all great men who successfully carry out great works.' Of all his appointees by far the most notable was Pugin, officially designated head of wood carving but in effect in charge of all the remaining departments, save that of stone carving.

Words like 'remarkable' and 'unique' are frequently devalued by being overworked but it is impossible to exaggerate the singularity of Pugin's life or the importance of his contribution either to Gothic architecture in general or to the Houses of Parliament in particular. One of the most amazing things about his career was its brevity. When he died, physically burned out and mentally unhinged, at the age of forty in 1852, he had designed more than one hundred buildings, published eight major books and established a business for the production of metal work and stained glass windows from his own designs. He had also entered actively into religious and architectural controversy. Almost all of his work had been crowded into a period of little more than a decade—from the time he established his practice in 1835 until his health began to fail in 1846.

The New Palace from the Embankment, c. 1860

Pugin was born in 1812, the son of Augustus Charles Pugin, himself an architect, archaeologist and architectural artist, who had been born in France and settled in England during the Revolution. A watercolourist of some note and a friend of many of the leading artists of the day, his main claim to fame stemmed from his association with Nash, and from his work as an illustrator of Gothic architecture. His drawings were models of clarity and he 'paved the way for the systematic study of detail which was the basis of that true (Gothic) revival.' Augustus Welby Pugin was early involved in his father's work. He showed a precociousness that was staggering. Before he was thirteen he was accompanying his father on foreign visits. By the time he was fifteen he had received a commission to design furniture for Windsor Castle. His twin passions were Gothic architecture and sailing—'there is nothing worth living for but Christian architecture and a boat'. When he was eighteen he was shipwrecked off the Scottish coast and made his way to the home of the architect Gillespie Graham. It was an encounter which was to have interesting results, for it was Pugin who drew Graham's entry for the Palace of Westminster competition.

He was married at the age of eighteen but his wife died in childbirth within the year and he was shortly afterward imprisoned for debt. On his release he set up a workshop for architectural accessories and drawings, specializing in metal-work designs. He married again in 1833 and soon afterwards established himself in business in Salisbury. About the same time he became a convert to Roman Catholicism, a conversion inspired by aesthetic as well as religious convictions. Pugin believed, with a dogmatic fervour that earned a strong rebuke from Cardinal Newman, that Roman Catholicism and Gothic art were intimately associated. 'He sees nothing good in any school of Christian art except that of which he is himself so great an ornament. The canons of Gothic architecture are to him points of faith and everyone is a heretic who would venture to question him.'

Pugin's association with Barry began in 1835 when he was employed by him to work on some of the decorative details for the King Edward VI Grammar School in Birmingham, one of Barry's most important commissions to date. There was no question of Pugin's taking over the design. Barry had been working on it for two years and evidence shows that it was virtually finished several months before he recruited Pugin. However, Barry felt that he needed details—roof bosses, pendants, ceiling decorations, spandrels and furniture—to complement his buildings, and these were the things in which Pugin excelled.

Both men were so satisfied with the collaboration that it was understandable that Barry should enlist Pugin's services when he decided to do everything possible to win the commission for the new Palace of Westminster. Architects frequently employed a competent assistant to help with the drawings of details and indeed Pugin's major contribution to the competition at this stage was the work that he did for Gillespie Graham whose entry he seems to have drawn almost entirely.

Nevertheless he also helped Barry, and when the competition was over and the award Barry's, it was natural that he should turn to the young genius with whom he had worked so successfully. He came to rely very heavily upon his expertise.

There is, however, no reason to doubt that Barry remained in overall control of the operation. We know, for instance, that he was responsible for the many revisions in the design for the gates to the House of Lords; that he called for corrections in the design submitted by Hardman for chandeliers in the Peers' library. That he had no cause to question or reject Pugin's work does not mean that he did not closely supervise it. Equally it does not mean that Pugin worked to the most detailed of briefs. The two would confer closely and Pugin would

The Waiting Lobby with the stairs to the Committee floor, c. 1845.

then be responsible for producing drawings, and manufacturing instructions, in harmony with the agreed solution. His creative talents were thus given rein. He united technical and stylistic knowledge and devised the ingenious adaptations of late medieval ornamental detail to nineteenth-century use, often having to work, as for instance on umbrella stands, inkwells, clocks, calendars and wallpapers, without any medieval model on which to base his designs.

The most splendid monument to Pugin's technical achievement within the Palace is undoubtedly the interior of the House of Lords but in the words of a most sympathetic biographer, 'The Houses of Parliament would not have been successful if it had not been for the commanding imagination and taste of Charles Barry, who recognized and understood the nature of Pugin's gift, nurtured its power, and provided an opportunity for its expression.'

They were, therefore, true collaborators and although each was of difficult temperament they worked remarkably smoothly together during the period from 1835 until 1838 and again from 1844 until Pugin collapsed in 1852. It was strange, therefore, that on Pugin's death Barry should have refused an invitation to act as a Trustee to administer the pension that was awarded to Pugin's third wife and his children. Why this should have been so, or why Barry should have apparently made no contact at all with the family, will always remain a mystery. It was not as if he had severed his relationship with Pugin himself. Almost up to the moment of Pugin's death he had written affectionate letters of solicitude.

Perhaps he was squeamish about publicly admitting his indebtedness to a man who died insane, but that sounds an improbable explanation of his conduct. Whatever the reason the Pugin family, and especially Edward Pugin, the elder son, smarted under the treatment and in 1860 Edward sought an interview with Barry claiming that he had evidence in the form of letters showing just how dependent Barry had been upon his father. Barry apparently received Edward Pugin courteously, although he asked to retain the letters, but matters did not come to a conclusion for Barry died three months later.

Another seven years elapsed and then Edward produced a pamphlet entitled 'Who was the Art Architect of the Houses of Parliament?' in which he sought to demonstrate that the true creative genius behind the building that was now the admiration of the world was his father. The Reverend Alfred Barry, third son of Sir Charles, entered a rejoinder, 'The Architect of the New Palace of Westminster', and then Edward Pugin continued the battle with 'Notes on Dr Barry's reply to the Infatuated Statement made by E.W.P.'

It was a sad business, made all the sadder by the fact that Barry had never sought to hide his dependence upon, or admiration for, Pugin when they had been working together, and by the fact that the controversy raged after both men were dead. Perhaps the fairest way one can summarize it is to stress that Pugin himself never claimed authorship, nor did Barry hide his reliance on Pugin's genius. But that it was Barry's overall conception and design there can be no doubt, nor was there at the time.

Recognition of Barry's work, however, was rather churlishly expressed at the time of his sudden death. The flag on the Victoria Tower flew at half-mast but less than a dozen Members of the Commons and Lords together subscribed barely fifty pounds towards the statue of the architect which it was agreed should stand within his masterpiece. When it was erected it was put not in a position of prominence or particular honour but tucked out of sight of visitors in the Lower Waiting Room to the Committee Floor of the Commons.

The treatment Barry received was echoed in that accorded to his son, Edward, who was appointed architect to the Palace after his father's death. The appointment itself was an inspired one, for Edward, the second of Barry's talented sons, had been intimately associated with his father's work in the Palace for many years and had an unrivalled knowledge of its construction. Furthermore he had been left all his father's drawings and papers relating to the building.

Although in 1860 the Palace looked much as it does today there was still a great deal of detailed work to be done and Edward Barry devoted most of his time for the next ten years to its achievement. His was the hand behind much of the decoration in the Royal Robing Room. He inspired the restoration of St Stephen's Crypt in which every inch of wall space in the old Chapel, now restored to religious use, was richly adorned. He was responsible too for the completion of the Royal staircase and of the cloisters and his most notable work on the exterior is the colonnade on the East side of New Palace Yard, built of Portland stone.

However, following the publication of Edward Pugin's attack, Edward Barry, whose relations with Parliament had been remarkably smooth hitherto, suddenly found himself the target of unwarranted criticism. In 1870, following an acrimonious correspondence with the Office of Works, he was dismissed from his post, having been ordered to surrender the drawings he had inherited and on which he was working towards the Palace's completion.

Whatever the reasons for Edward Barry's totally unexpected and unjustified dismissal—there were suggestions that it was because of alarm at the already noticeable decaying of the stone work (hardly his fault), or because of the Pugin controversy—when he left Westminster in 1870 almost all *was* complete except for a major scheme which he had submitted for a redesigned Chamber for the Commons. Save for installing more frescoes and statues, and work in the twentieth century designed to replace the decayed or destroyed, or to care for the extra needs of Members, the Palace is as Edward Barry left it. It is in most essentials, and to all outside appearances, the Palace we know today.

CHAPTER FIVE

The Palace Described

Earth has not anything to show more fair;
Dull would he be of soul who could pass by
A sight so touching in its majesty:

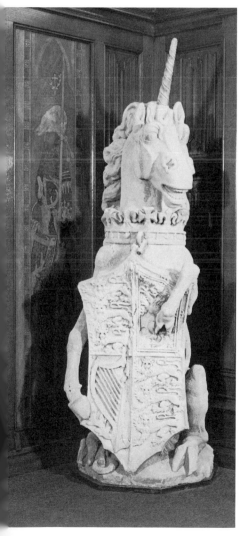

One of the original heraldic beasts, now preserved inside the Palace.

WORDSWORTH wrote these lines 'Composed upon Westminster Bridge' in 1802. In 1870 most Londoners would have though them a fitting description of their great new Palace, and there have been few in the years since the younger Barry's death in 1880 who would have quarrelled with those sentiments. Pugin, passing the rising Palace as he journeyed down the Thames in the mid '40's, turned to his companion and remarked, 'All Grecian, Sir: Tudor details on a classic body.' But the architect's disparaging verdict (and there could be no clearer disclaimer of responsibility for the design) has been shared by very few. Nicholas I of Russia thought it 'a dream in stone'; the French architect, Lassus, 'a fairy Palace, a marvel of the Thousand and One Nights.'

In our own day Lord Clark has called the Houses of Parliament, 'A triumph of the Picturesque . . . No painter can resist them', and certainly no building has inspired more artists in the last century. It is not difficult to appreciate why.

Seen in any light, and from any angle, Barry's Palace always has a magic of its own. From Lambeth, breaking through the mists of an early May morning, it seems to float upon the waters, and seen from the same spot in the gloom of a late November afternoon it looms massive and majestic. Whether you see it in these romantic or haunting lights and from this, the very best of vantage points, or look across from Westminster Bridge on a brilliant summer's afternoon, or on a still black night, when its rooms are ablaze with light and the lantern atop Big Ben tells that the House is still at its work; or whether you approach it from the landward side walking between the Abbey and St Margaret's suddenly to be confronted by its West Front with the statue of Richard I prominent in the foreground of Old Palace Yard, you cannot help but be captivated by the place.

It is, by any standards, a great building. From afar it has much of the glory, and not a little of the mystery, of our very finest cathedrals. And, as with those cathedrals, the visitor is not disappointed when he arrives. There is a wealth of detail to ponder at and to admire and there is a theme and a discipline which ensures that the statuary and other enrichment impresses but does not overwhelm. Even the grime

109

of a century, which has robbed it of much of the golden glow that Barry intended, has not detracted from its beauty, though it is to be hoped that Parliament will at last take action to clean its home, and that it will not continue to shirk the task through notions of false economy. As a noticeably strict Liberal economist remarked during one of the interminable debates on the building and the estimates over a century ago, 'That was not economy but scandalous parsimony which grudged what was necessary to support our national monuments.' *Plus ca change*!

Today's visitor sees the Palace much as the elder Barry designed it and left it, though without the extension (or 'completion' as he preferred to call it) which would have enclosed New Palace Yard and provided a grand entrance at the corner of Bridge Street and Parliament Square, close by where the statue of Sir Winston Churchill now stands. There have, however, been structural alterations to the Palace. In 1941 the Commons chamber was destroyed and had to be rebuilt. The opportunity of providing some extra accommodation was taken and there have been further additions in Star Chamber Court and elsewhere since. None of these, however, is visible from outside.

Inside, the wear of time on imperfectly chosen materials has led to the disappearance of a number of the original frescoes, and the shattering of the air raids destroyed most of the original stained glass. Some rooms have had their uses changed and others their furniture moved. But here again the Palace, in spite of the developments of democracy over more than a century, remains much as Barry and Pugin left it, and new visitors are just as impressed by its size and grandeur as those who attended the first State Opening by Queen Victoria in 1852.

To try and reduce such a building to a list of figures, or to seek to convey its flavour by a dull recital of facts, is an insult to the imagination, but an understanding of the size of the place is essential if we are to appreciate the sheer physical achievements of those who designed and built it, and to admire what they created.

It is by any standards an enormous building. It covers an area of eight acres and the whole pile rests on a vast bed of concrete— necessary because of the nature of the ground on which it was built— as much as ten and a half feet thick. The North Front, which stretches from the river to the Clock Tower is 232 feet in length, and the South (from the Victoria Tower to the river) 322 feet. Each posed a problem for the architect but it was as nothing compared with the challenge presented by the length of the river front to the east. This is 872 feet long, the Terrace taking up 678 feet. It is one of the marks of Barry's genius that he was able to create this enormous facade without making it either dull to behold, or difficult to live with. Perhaps the greatest tribute to his success has been the continuing popularity of the Terrace. An invitation to take tea there is as eagerly received by the constituents of a Socialist mining MP today as it was by the

110

The Palace of Westminster: the classic view from Lambeth.

debutantes who paraded their charms there at the turn of the century.

It is from the Terrace that one can most readily appreciate the vastness of the building. Commons and Lords together contain something over 1,110 rooms (ranging from the smallest office to the Royal Gallery) 126 staircases, 35 lifts (not allowed for by Barry, of course) and two miles of corridors. There are, furthermore, a series of 11 courtyards behind the river front, with a carriageway running through them which connects Speaker's Court in the north (the Commons occupies the whole of the northern part of the building) with the Royal Court in the south.

No visitor on the Terrace, surveying the carved inscriptions,

enrichments and statues, is surprised to learn that there are over 300 major statues on the main facade alone (mostly saints and sovereigns, from Alfred to Victoria) or to be told that three-quarters of a million cubic feet of stone were used in the building. The stone is, with the exception of the Younger Barry's colonnade in the New Palace Yard, mostly magnesian limestone from Anston in Yorkshire. Sadly the Bolsover stone which Barry wanted to use was not available in sufficient quantities, and what was eventually chosen has not proved very suitable for withstanding the assaults of the London air.

Not visible from the Terrace are the three towers which give the Palace so much of its grace and dignity and are themselves architectural achievements of a high order. The Clock Tower rises 316 feet above the river, the Central Tower, built to accommodate Dr Reid's scheme, is 300 feet high, whilst the Victoria Tower (planned as the King's Tower when it was designed in the reign of William IV) is 323 feet high to the base of its enormous flagstaff.

Perhaps the most difficult fact for today's inflation-conscious visitor to absorb is that the whole Palace cost well under three million pounds to build *and* to furnish. This was about the same sum that was needed to rebuild the Commons Chamber between 1948 and 1951, and rather less than the cost of the underground car park which was constructed in the early 1970's under New Palace Yard.

The visitor does not see more than the entrance to that remarkable feat of modern engineering but, as costly and controversial as its construction was, it does serve as a reminder that the Palace is very much a working institution. Apart from the six hundred and thirty five Members of Parliament there are four hundred or more Peers who regularly attend the Upper House, and almost two thousand people employed in this great 'workship of democracy': clerks and librarians, police and custodians, chefs and messengers, engineers and cleaners, the staff of the House of Commons Post Office and secretaries and accountants. The visitor sees few of them or few of the places where they work. He does, however, have the chance of seeing the Chamber and some of the great rooms and corridors on the Principal Floor, a Committee at work in one of Barry's river-front Committee Rooms on the first floor, and, sometimes, if the guest of a Member or Peer, of taking a meal in one of the dining rooms where Strangers (and every visitor, however exalted, is a 'stranger') are allowed.

Most visitors who come to tour the Palace come in by the Sovereign's Entrance to the House of Lords. For the first part of their tour they follow the route the Queen takes when she comes to read the speech from the throne at the State Opening of Parliament. In recent years, save for the 'austerity opening' after the crisis election in 1974 when the nation was in the middle of great industrial trouble, the State Opening has been the same glittering occasion it was when Queen Victoria first drove under the great arch at the bottom of the Victoria Tower in 1852. The Queen does just the same, arriving in the Irish State Coach with an escort of the Household Cavalry, following a

procession of state carriages in which are conveyed the crown, the maces and other regalia associated with this, the most colourful and symbolic of our annual ceremonial state occasions.

The Sovereign's Entrance is then at the very southern end of the building in Old Palace Yard, as it is still called. Here was the great court of the Old Palace, Standing at the entrance one looks west to Westminster Abbey and the glorious Henry VII Chapel. Almost immediately opposite is one of the few remnants of the Old Palace, the small Jewel Tower. Built during the reign of Edward III to house his privy treasure, it was used for over two hundred years, until the latter part of the nineteenth century, to store parliamentary records. This is now the function of the Victoria Tower. Here are kept three million Parliamentary documents, including the master copies of every Act passed by Parliament since the end of the fifteenth century. The Record Office was completely reconstructed between 1948 and 1963 and consists of twelve air-conditioned floors with a total area of over 32,000 square feet and five and a half miles of steel shelving. Any serious researcher or amateur historian can consult the records of Parliamentary history: Journals of the House, minutes of Select Committee's meetings, Parliamentary Petitions, and a whole range of other manuscripts and printed documents.

When the House is sitting the Union Jack flies from the flagstaff at the top of the Tower from 10.00 am until sunset; and when the Sovereign comes it is replaced by the Royal Standard. The ordinary visitor does not see the archway, decorated with the statues of the patron saints (and presided over by a lifesize statue of Queen Victoria, flanked by figures of Justice and Mercy) through which the Queen passes. But he does have a chance to walk up Barry's imposing Royal Staircase with its unbroken ascent of wide stairs, specially designed for easy mounting, and later enriched by Edward Barry with marble and mosaic.

Immediately inside the Palace you are conscious of Barry's intent to create 'a sculptured memorial of our national history'. Indeed as you wander through the Palace you are constantly reminded of this didactic purpose. In this, as in so much else, Barry and Pugin were consciously following the Gothic tradition of those who built our cathedrals and great parish churches, and who needed, through the medium of stained glass, sculpture and wall painting, to teach an illiterate congregation the basic tenets of their faith. This was to be the greatest of all secular cathedrals and those who had the privilege of living in an emerging democracy under a reformed Parliament were to have constant reminders of the growth of their country's greatness, and of its constitution, when they visited its senate house.

At the top of the Royal Staircase is the Norman Porch. This was the intended place for the statues of our Norman Kings but they have never been put there. The name alone remains. Today there are portraits of King William IV, in whose reign the old Palace was destroyed, and of the great Duke of Wellington, while all around are

The Clock Tower and Speaker's House from Westminster Bridge.

busts of eighteenth- and nineteenth-century Prime Ministers, including the elder Pitt, Palmerston and Disraeli.

The porch serves as an ante-room to one of the finest Gothic apartments in England, the Royal Robing Rooms. It was not completed until 1866 and owes much to Edward Barry who was responsible for the richly inlaid floor with its heraldic devices of portcullis, rose and lion, and the remarkably ornate chimney piece with its figures of St George on either side: on the right hand the saint is fighting the dragon and on the left he has it dead at his feet. Patriotic chivalry is indeed the theme of the room, for around the walls are five frescoes by Dyce illustrating the knightly virtues of generosity, religion, courtesy, mercy and hospitality with scenes from the Arthurian legends. There were to have been seven, but Dyce, working on wet plaster and painting only in the summer, died before he had completed the commission. Beneath the pictures and above the oak dado are eighteen carved panels by Armstead, again showing scenes from the legends of King Arthur, the last one, by the door to the Norman Porch, showing Arthur borne away by the Queen to Avalon. Around the room are superbly carved Gothic chairs, and at the east end, on a stepped dais and beneath a canopy carved with thistle, rose and shamrock, and the royal cipher, a chair of state. At the back of the dais are the Royal Arms on a background of royal ciphers, worked by women from the Royal School of Needlework in 1856. You are always conscious of Victoria in this incredibly rich room, and on either side of the chair are Winterhalter's portraits of the Queen and her Consort.

After the destruction of the Chamber of the Commons in 1941 the Lords met in the Robing Room. Tiers of benches were installed and a gallery built for reporters and strangers. Here, until the Lords returned to their own Chamber in May, 1951, the business of the Upper House was conducted.

The Robing Room has recently been thoroughly restored and now stands as it did when first completed, containing within it some of the finest work of two men who worked more closely than perhaps any others with Barry and Pugin: Hardman, who was responsible for the metal work of the chimney piece and the doors, and Crace, who decorated the splendidly ornate ceiling.

The Robing Room opens on to the Royal Gallery, one of the grandest and most imposing rooms in the whole Palace. One hundred and ten feet long, forty-five feet wide and forty-five feet high it is, in effect, a grand processional hall between the Robing Room and the Chamber of the Lords, although it has been the scene of some notable Parliamentary events. Here Lord Russell was tried by his Peers for bigamy in 1901 and sent to prison for three months and Lord de Clifford was acquitted on a manslaughter charge in 1935, the last nobleman to be tried by his Peers (the right was abolished in 1948). Addresses from both Houses of Parliament were presented to King George V in November, 1918, after the signing of the Armistice, and to George VI at the end of the European and Japanese wars. Visiting Heads of State have addressed both Houses here on a number of occasions in recent years, and in 1972 the Privy Council gave a banquet in celebration of the Queen's Silver Wedding.

For these functions the Royal Gallery is a suitably sumptuous setting, with its fine ceiling, its floor of encaustic tiles designed by Pugin and produced by Minton, and the gilded statues of Alfred, William the Conqueror, Richard I, Edward III, Henry V, Queen Elizabeth, William III, and Queen Anne, (all by Birnie Philip) standing guard around.

The statues act as companions to a series of royal portraits depicting most of our kings and queens from George I to Elizabeth II. The pity is that so many of them are indifferent works of art.

The dominating pictures in the room, however, are far from indifferent. These are two enormous frescoes painted by Daniel Maclise, between 1858 and 1865. They show the most dramatic moments of those two great victories over France which established Britain's supremacy at the beginning of the last century: Nelson shot on the quarterdeck of the *Victory* at Trafalgar in 1805 and Wellington greeting Marshal Blücher on the battlefield of Waterloo ten years later. The pictures are forty-five feet long and twelve feet high and they are by far the most outstanding pictures painted for the Palace. Unlike most historical narrative pictures they pulsate with life and the accuracy with which every minute detail has been observed is

The river front from Westminster Bridge. Note the Central Tower—originally constructed to house a ventilating shaft.

115

astonishing: it is small wonder that engravings of Maclise's
masterpieces found their way into almost every Victorian school-
room. As T. S. R. Boase, one of the foremost authorities on English art
wrote, 'There is much carnage but there is also compassion ...
English art in the high, romantic vein, has seldom reached such
narrative power and found such force and range to set it out.'

From the Royal Gallery you pass into the Prince's Chamber, a small
ante-room to the Chamber of the House of Lords. There is no
particular significance in its name; it was chosen to remind us that
there was a Prince's Chamber next to the House of Lords in the Old
Palace. This is almost the only room in the Palace that can be
described as a disappointment. Ceiling, wainscoting and furniture
are of a standard to rank with any other and the two octagonal tables
designed by Pugin are among his best furniture. Around the walls are
a series of Tudor portraits painted in the 1850's by students of the
Royal School of Art in South Kensington, depicting on one side Henry

Left: *Sauntering on the Terrace In Edwardian times.*

Right: *The Terrace today.*

VII and his wife, Prince Arthur and Catherine of Aragon, and Henry, the brother who succeeded Arthur as Prince of Wales, and his six wives. There are Henry's children and, on the west side of the room a further series of portraits including Mary Queen of Scots, Francis II of France, her first husband, and Lord Darnley, her second. Above the portraits is an elaborately carved armorial frieze and below a series of bronze bas-reliefs commemorating some of the more notable events of the Tudor period such as the Field of the Cloth of Gold, Raleigh spreading his cloak before Queen Elizabeth, the death of Sir Philip Sidney and the murder of Rizzio. What mars the room, however, is a massive statue of Queen Victoria in juvenile puddingy majesty by John Gibson. Seen at a distance in one of the royal parks it might just pass but here it is incongruous and destructive of the atmosphere.

It is quickly forgotten as you enter the Chamber of the House of Lords. Alfred Barry, the architect's third son and biographer, tells us that Barry considered the House of Lords 'not a mere place of business nor even a mere House of Lords—but as a Chamber in which a Sovereign, surrounded by the Court, summoned the three estates of the realm'. Few would question his accomplishment in translating vision into reality. Here he and Pugin, who was responsible for almost all the enriching and adorning of the Chamber, created their masterpiece. At the southern end, surrounded by a brass rail, is the throne, which, with Pugin's great standing candelabra on each side, and his exquisitely carved and gilded canopy above, combines splendour and elegance in high degree and is the focal point of the most richly appointed legislative Chamber in the world.

At the State Opening of Parliament the brass rail is removed and two thrones installed under the canopy, one for the Queen and the other for the Duke of Edinburgh. In the compartments on either side sit the Prince of Wales and Princess Anne.

When the Lords is in session Privy Councillors and the eldest sons of Peers are allowed to sit on the steps of the throne and therefore just behind the other great seat in the Chamber, the Woolsack. This large, squat, red-covered seat serves as a reminder that in the Middle Ages England's prosperity depended on the wool trade. Since the reign of Edward III the Lord Chancellor has taken his seat on the woolsack. Today the stuffing is still of wool, from the four constituent countries of the United Kingdom and from the Commonwealth. At the front of the Lord Chancellor's are two other long woolsacks where the Lords of Appeal in their judicial robes sit at the State Opening of Parliament.

The Chamber of the House of Lords.

They emphasize the twin functions, legislative and judicial, of the House of Lords, and the fact that it is the highest court in the land. The Chancellor himself embodies these twin functions. His is the senior judicial figure in the country and he also acts as Speaker of the House of Lords. Unlike the Speaker of the House of Commons, the Lord Chancellor is a political figure with a senior place in the Cabinet and he sometimes speaks on behalf of the Government in the Chamber, though when he does so he must stand aside from the woolsack.

Immediately to the right of the Lord Chancellor, on the red leather-upholstered benches, sit the Bishops. Twenty-six Lords Spiritual have been entitled to sit in the House of Lords since the Reformation; to the early Parliaments Bishops and mitred Abbots were summoned. The two Archbishops and the Bishops of London, Winchester and Durham take their seats as of right. The other twenty-one Bishops sit by virtue of their seniority of appointment. Thus a newly appointed Bishop of Lincoln may wait several years before taking his seat in the Lords despite the importance of his See. Beyond the Bishops, and still on the Chancellor's right sit the Government Peers, whilst on his left are the Opposition parties.

Below the table of the House, at which the three Clerks sit, are the Cross Benches, a feature unique to the House of Lords. On these Benches sit the Royal Dukes and others who cannot, or do not wish to, proclaim any party allegiance (retired but ennobled Archbishops and senior civil servants for instance).

Beyond the Cross Benches is the Bar of the House to which the Commons, led by their Speaker, are summoned to hear the speech from the throne at the State Opening of Parliament, and the reading of the Queen's Commission when Parliament is dissolved or prorogued. The attendance of the Commons at the Bar of the Lords reminds us that Parliament was once a single assembly—the King 'in Parliament assembled', with Lords and Commons present together.

Pugin lavished great care on the Chamber of the Upper House. Nothing was too small to escape his attention. One of his most notable pieces of furniture is here: the table at which the Clerks sit. The ceiling of the House is one of his finest works, divided into eighteen compartments and adorned with the ancient badges of our kings, the white hart of Richard II, the sun of York, the crown in the bush (Henry VII), the lion passant of England, the lion rampant of Scotland, the harp of Ireland, the Tudor rose, the pomegranate of Castile, the lily of France, the portcullis of Beaufort. Unfortunately the original stained glass windows, like most in the Palace, were shattered in the Second World War. They have been replaced by a series bearing the coats of arms of peers from 1360 to 1900.

Between the windows at the end of the Chamber are bronze figures of the eighteen barons who compelled John to set his seal to Magna Carta, and under the side galleries carved oak pillars surmounted by

119

busts of English Kings. Behind the throne are three frescoes: Edward III conferring the Order of the Garter on the Black Prince; the baptism of St Ethelbert; Prince Henry (later Henry V) acknowledging the authority of Judge Gascoigne. Behind the Strangers' Gallery are three more depicting the spirits of Justice, Religion and Chivalry, two of them by Maclise. In the Lords the Press Gallery is at the northern end, facing the woolsack and above the Bar of the House, and there, discreetly tucked away, is the commentary box from which the sound broadcasts of the Lords in session are transmitted.

On either side of the Chamber are voting lobbies. Unlike the Commons, where there is a fairly elaborate ritual of voting 'Aye' or 'No', Peers vote 'Content' or 'Not Content' merely by going into the lobbies and having their names registered as they do so.

It was in this Chamber that some of Churchill's greatest speeches were made, after the Commons was destroyed in 1941 and the Lords adjourned to the Robing Room.

Though the move made every sense from the point of view of convenience, it also underlined the supremacy of the Lower House in terms of political power and importance. No Member of the Lords has held the Premiership since Lord Salisbury in 1902, and, whatever reforms or changes may overtake the Upper House, there is little chance of his losing that particular claim to fame. Since 1964 all new Peerages have been life peerages, created under the Act of 1958, but hereditary peers still have the right to sit in the Lords, and a very large number of them exercise it and are conscientious and regular in their attendances. Because the conferring of a peerage is generally for services rendered for a lifetime of distinguished work outside the House most of the younger Members of the Lords are, in fact, hereditary peers.

In spite of the fact that the Commons is now politically far more important than the Lords, the constitutional supremacy of the Lords is marked in a number of quaint ways. The Lords is always referred to as the Upper House and the Clerk to the House of Lords is the Clerk to the Parliaments, just as the Chamber of the Lords is more properly, although very rarely, described as the Parliament Chamber. This is because the Lords is the place where the constituent elements of Parliament, (Monarch, Lords and Commons) meet together, and the superiority of the Lords at these ceremonial meetings is marked by the fact that the Peers sit while the Members of the Commons merely stand at the Bar.

To get there they come in procession through the Peers' Lobby into which the visitor to the Lords passes when he leaves the Chamber. Through this Lobby too, the Lord Chancellor comes in procession, preceded by the Serjeant-At-Arms bearing the Mace, at the beginning of each sitting. The door through which he passes into the Chamber is the finest feature of the Lobby. Made by Hardman, who was responsible for so much of the metalwork in the Palace, it is of solid brass. The encaustic tiling of the floor is a further reminder of

The Peers' Lobby, showing Hardman's brass doors into the Chamber.

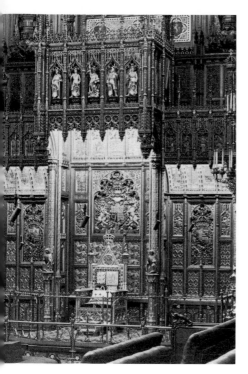

The canopy over the Throne in the House of Lords—Pugin's masterpiece.

Pugin. With its Tudor rose centrepiece in enamel and brass it is one of the loveliest floors, and one of the best preserved, in the Palace.

One of the features which gives a special richness to the Lords apartments is the red leather in which all benches and chairs are covered. You notice it in the Peers' Corridor, which leads from the Peers' Lobby to the Central Lobby, where it abruptly changes and you find the seats henceforth upholstered in a rather dingy green. There is great historical significance in these colours. Red, the traditional colour of royalty, has been associated with the Lords since at least the beginning of the sixteenth century and the use of green as the predominant colour in the Commons furnishing dates from the middle of the seventeenth century at the very latest.

When the new House of Lords was first occupied the praise heaped upon Barry and Pugin was ecstatic: 'Without doubt the finest example of Gothic civil architecture in Europe ... Its proportions, arrangements and decorations are perfect. The size and loftiness of the apartment, its finely proportioned windows, with the gilded and canopied niches between them; the throne glowing with golden colours; the richly carved panelling that lines the walls, with its gilded and emblazoned cove, and the balcony of brass rising from the canopy; the roof most elaborately painted; its massive beams and sculptured ornaments and pendants richly gilded; all unite in forming a scene of royal magnificence as brilliant as it is unequalled.'

Because of the destruction of the Commons Chamber and Lobby in 1941, it is to the southern end of the Palace that we have to look to be aware of the greatest triumphs achieved by the Barry/Pugin collaboration, and it is in the Chamber of the House of Lords itself that we see their work at its best. There is a richness and an opulence which never degenerates into flamboyance or vulgarity. As James Pope-Hennessy wrote, 'The ceiling of the Lords, in fact, was decorated in severest conformity with Barry's favourite maxim—that "tawdriness" was only produced by "half measures" and that if you intended to use gold you should use it thoroughly. Together with the encrusted canopy of the royal throne, this ceiling can be looked upon as the climax or apogee of Augustus Welby Pugin's achievement in the Palace of Westminster.'

Along the Peers' Corridor is a series of paintings by C. W. Cope illustrating some of the more significant events of the Stuart period: Lord Russell taking leave of his wife before going to his execution; the embarkation of the Pilgrim Fathers in 1620: the burial of Charles I at Windsor. However, the most interesting and most significant, from a Parliamentary point of view, is undoubtedly that showing Speaker Lenthall asserting the privileges of the Commons before Charles I on the occasion of the King's visit to arrest the five Members. It does not rank with Maclise's great work in the Royal Gallery but it is one of the more successful narrative historical pictures in the Palace and one which, for understandable reasons, has endeared itself to generations of Members of Parliament showing their constituents around.

Those constituents, and indeed all British subjects, have right of access to the next great apartment of the Palace, into which the Peers' Corridor leads: the Central Lobby.

Barry planned the Palace of Westminster so that all of the main Chambers and lobbies to which Members of the Commons and Peers needed to have access were on one principal floor, with a central corridor running through the building from Lords to Commons. It is thus possible to stand before the throne in the House of Lords and look directly down through the Peers' Lobby and corridor and beyond to the Speaker's Chair in the Commons.

The Central Lobby or, as it is more properly called, the Central Hall of the Palace of Westminster, is the hub of Barry's design. It is also the hub of activity of the Palace. Here the Commons begins, and here visitors and constituents come to meet their MPs, or to 'lobby' them for a specific cause. One of the distinguishing features of the British system of Parliamentary Government is the constituency system. Every British subject is represented by a Member of Parliament and is entitled, irrespective of voting records or intentions, to see that Member within the precincts of the Palace of Westminster.

The Lobby itself is a fitting centre for a great Parliament. It is octagonal, like some great Cathedral Chapter House, but there is no central pillar to obstruct the view or progress of Members or visitors. The vaulted roof is seventy-five feet high and the ribs which fan out from the pillars at the side are joined by 250 elaborately carved and beautifully coloured bosses, the spaces between them filled with gilded and sparkling Venetian mosaics. Barry had planned that it should be yet higher, but Dr Reid's demand for the central tower for his ventilating system obliged the architect to lower the roof.

In the centre of the lobby hangs a great brass chandelier, like the door to the House of Lords the work of John Hardman. Again, as in the Lords' Lobby, there is a Minton tiled floor with a Latin inscription in the centre which, translated, reads, 'Except the Lord build the House they labour in vain that build it.' (Psalm 127). There are four great archways which give on to the various parts of the Palace. To the south is the Lords and to the north the Commons. In the west is the public entrance to the House of Commons through St Stephen's Hall, and to the east the corridor that leads to the dining rooms and libraries, and the staircase to the Committee Floor. On either side of each archway are niches with statues of Kings and Queens of England; above the doorways are mosaic panels depicting the four patron saints. Over the north door is St David with his Bishop's Cross and a dove alighting on his shoulder, on each side an angel, one carrying a harp symbolizing harmony, and on the other the lamp of light. Opposite is St George, the dragon at his feet with Fortitude carrying his banner in her hand, while Purity stands to the left bearing his helmet and a bunch of white lilies. These mosaics were designed by Edward Poynter and installed in the last decades of the nineteenth century, having been executed in Venice by Salviati. The

The intricate design and decoration of the ceiling in the Central Lobby.

Lord Granville guards the Central Lobby Post Office.

Hardman's great brass chandelier in the Central Lobby.

Right: *The Central Lobby.*

other panels were not filled until 1923. Both were designed by Anning Bell and created in situ. Over the east door is St Andrew with his staff and his fishing net, the saltire behind him, and St Margaret of Scotland on the left with a bible and a black cross, the Holy Rood of Scotland containing in its central reliquary a portion of the True Cross. On the Saint's right is St Mungo, founder of the See of Glasgow. Over the west door is St Patrick wearing the robes of a Bishop with the Rock of Cashel behind him and the shamrock at his feet. On his right is St Columbus representing the north of Ireland, with the red hand of Ulster on the shield at his feet; on his left St Bridget above an Irish harp.

Around the Lobby are large marble statues of four prominent statesmen of the last century: Earl Russell, Sir Stafford Northcote, Lord Granville and Mr Gladstone.

Along the Commons Corridor are more frescoes of notable seventeenth century incidents, this time by E. M. Ward. The most famous one, already referred to, shows Charles II landing at Dover in 1660 with one of the reception committee bearing a Union Jack—a full forty-seven years before any version of the flag came into being. Others are of Charles escaping after the Battle of Worcester, Montrose being led to execution, the last sleep of Argyll before his execution and, most significant in a Parliamentary context, General Monk declaring for a free Parliament, and Parliament offering the Crown to William and Mary.

The Commons Corridor leads into the Commons, or Members'

Lobby. This is rather larger than the Lords' Lobby and, as if in preparation for the Chamber to which it leads, more austere. Nevertheless it is bright and light and, when the House is sitting, a hive of activity. Then no members of the public are admitted. The only ones who can frequent the Lobby are Members themselves, members of the staff of the House and the Lobby correspondents who are attached to the various national and local papers, or to one of the television or radio stations. Here Members may talk to journalists on 'Lobby terms', giving them information without fear of attribution, on which the journalists can base their accounts of what 'Parliament is thinking', and write their speculative pieces about the outcome of some imminent and crucial vote.

As with the Central Lobby there are four doorways, one leading to the Chamber, another to the Members' Entrance, the third to the Central Lobby and the fourth to the libraries and dining rooms.

The Lobby was badly damaged when the Chamber was destroyed in 1941, and a constant reminder of this is the battle-scarred, bomb-damaged archway, over the door into the Chamber. It was Churchill's suggestion that the arch was kept thus, 'as a monument to the ordeal that Parliament has passed through in the Great War, and as a reminder to those who will come centuries after that they may look back from time to time upon their forebears, "who kept the bridge in the brave days of old".'

The arch is known now as the Churchill arch, and by its side, massively brooding, is Oscar Nemon's great bronze statue of Sir Winston, unveiled in 1969. On the right of the arch is a statue of David Lloyd George, Prime Minister during the most crucial years of the First World War. Around the Lobby are other statues, this time in stone, of Joseph Chamberlain, Arthur Balfour and Asquith, and a further bronze of Clement Attlee unveiled by Lord Shinwell in December, 1979. There are two empty plinths.

To the right of the statue of Lloyd George is the Vote Office where Members collect their Parliamentary papers, and a little to the right of this the message board. Here internal mail for Members, letters from Government Departments and answers to Parliamentary Questions are left. On the other side of the Lobby is a similar board for telephone messages and telegrams. On either side of the doorway leading to the Chamber are chairs for the Doorkeepers. The Principal doorkeeper has the job of guarding the snuff box from which Members may demand a free pinch of snuff before entering the Chamber — a relic of the days when the air of the Chamber was less healthy and snuff a convenient means of clearing the nostrils and obliterating unpleasant odours.

These are the doors which are ceremoniously shut in the face of Black Rod, when he comes to deliver the summons for the Commons to attend in the Lords to hear the speech from the throne.

The Commons Chamber is very different from the one whence Black Rod comes. There is none of the arresting richness of the Lords here. This is, and looks like, a working Chamber; not a suitable setting

Winston Churchill and Lloyd George flank the Churchill Arch to the Commons' Chamber.

The Members' Post Office in the Commons' Lobby.

for formal or elaborate ceremony.

Of course, this is not the Chamber which Barry was obliged to alter and which, having done so, he never willingly entered again. This is not the scene of the great Gladstone—Disraeli duels, or whence Irish Members were forcibly removed on Mr Speaker's order. But of all the rooms in the Palace this was the one which Barry would most willingly have sacrificed. He would not have relished the thought of its always being known as 'Barry's Chamber', nor looked kindly upon those parliamentarians who insisted, almost without dissent, that what replaced it after its destruction on the night of 10 May, 1941, should be as near as possible to Barry's 'original'.

In fact the Chamber is very different in detail, if not in outline. The floor area (68 feet by 45 feet 6 inches) is exactly the same as before, but although Sir Giles Gilbert Scott followed his brief implicitly in designing the new Chamber in Gothic style, it is very much a subdued Gothic. He made no attempt to reproduce the elaborate designs of the old stonework, and in place of the ecclesiastical type windows Barry had inserted he designed simple mullioned ones of domestic type with clear glass. The most obvious difference is the woodwork. Scott used oak throughout, but in place of the former dark rich tones he had his Shropshire oak bleached to give it a lighter colour and so remove any vestigial traces of Victorian 'antiquity' or gloom. However, although this is the most apparent difference, the greatest change is in the galleries. Gone is the ladies gallery with the grille in front of it ('something between a birdcage and a tea caddy'), and in the changes made above the Chamber an extra 170 seats were provided for strangers and reporters, giving a total of 929 seats of which 427, as in the old Chamber, are for Members.

The Chamber of the House of Commons looking towards the Opposition Benches.

When the number of seats came to be determined there were echoes of the debates of the 1860's. Then Edward Barry had submitted a scheme which would have transformed the Chamber into a new and larger Members' Lobby and created a square and more commodious Chamber in the Commons' Court. His suggestion was for a Chamber of 63 feet square and 69 feet high which would have accommodated 419 Members on the floor and 150 in the gallery, together with 330 strangers and reporters. There had been pressure for such an extension, owing to the consistently high attendance at debates, but nothing came of the plan and, after the destruction in 1941, when it was again suggested that enlargement would be appropriate, the advocates of a small Chamber, which would not look empty when sparsley attended, but which would be crowded and have its atmosphere charged by the jostling proximity of hundreds of colleagues on great occasions, won the day. They were led by Churchill.

The Table of the House of Commons.

The roof is of the same general pattern as Barry's lowered roof was, rising from the sides towards the centre, though in the present Chamber the panels in the flat centre part of the roof are of glass, behind which is fluorescent lighting.

The benches are covered in green leather as before, and there are sound amplifiers in the shape of portcullises along the backs of the benches. Suspended from the ceiling are a number of microphones and, whatever the general hubbub, a Member can almost invariably tell what the speaker is saying if he puts his head back against the amplifier. A similar system operates in the Chamber of the Lords. It has given rise to many jests about Members being asleep—when in fact they have merely been straining to catch their colleagues' pearls of wisdom.

The carpet is also green but on either side of the Chamber, and running the length of it, are two thick red stripes. Traditionally these are supposed to be two swords' lengths apart to symbolize the fact that arguments here are resolved by debate and persuasion, rather than by more violent means. It is difficult to reconcile the tradition entirely with the rules that were known to pertain in the days when Members came into the House wearing swords. For they were obliged to leave them before entering the Chamber and even today every Member has a loop of pink tape for his sword attached to his coathanger in the Members' cloakroom—dozens of umbrellas drip there on wet days. One rule, however, is still very firm. No Member may address the

House in front of the red stripe. To 'overstep the mark' is to be 'out of order'.

At the north end of the Chamber, and dominating it, is the Speaker's Chair. Before the fire in 1834 this changed with each Speaker, for the Chair was one of the perquisites of office and when the Speaker retired, he was allowed to take it with him, just as he was allowed to take the silver provided for his use in his State dining room. Thus we find the Chair of Speaker Norton (1769–1780) in the London Museum, that of Speaker Abbot (1802–1816) in All Souls, Oxford and the canopy of the Chair occupied by Speaker Lenthall in Radleigh Church in Oxfordshire. Pugin's Chair, perhaps his finest piece of furniture and the greatest single loss of 1941, has now been replaced by a simple but dignified and massive chair, made of black bean wood from North Queensland. Inscribed on the back of the Chair is 'The Gift of Australia'.

When the Chamber was rebuilt all the dominions and colonies gave something towards its furnishing. Thus, Australia gave the Chair and Canada provided the table of the House which dominates the centre of the Chamber. From New Zealand came the bronze-bound dispatch boxes of Pururi wood, from which Government Ministers and Opposition spokesmen address the House. The three Clerks' chairs were given by South Africa, the Serjeant-at-Arms' chair by Ceylon, the entrance doors by India and Pakistan and the telescopic Bar of the House, to which offenders against its rites are summoned, by Jamaica. Rhodesia gave the copper rests on which the Mace is placed.

Above and behind the Speaker's Chair is the Press gallery, while facing it, and above the Bar of the House, are the main public galleries. In the south-west corner of the Chamber, below these, is the commentary box from which the proceedings are broadcast.

Almost the only decorations in the Chamber are the shields beneath the south gallery, emblazoned with the arms and initials of the nineteen Members who gave their lives during the First World War, and those under the north gallery which commemorate the twenty-three Members killed in the Second. In 1979 another crest was added, that of Airey Neave, the war hero who became Member for Abingdon and who was murdered by Irish fanatics in New Palace Yard.

Though the quality of debating in the House of Lords may often be higher and the contributions better informed and less partisan, this is the Chamber with which the public associate 'Parliament', and its proceedings have become disturbingly familiar as a result of the broadcasting of Question Time and major statements since April, 1978. Broadcasting, however, has not been allowed to alter the pattern of Parliamentary business, nor the essentials of parliamentary procedure. Still each day's sitting begins (2.30 pm from Monday to Thursday and 9.30 am on Fridays) with the Speaker processing through the Central Lobby and the Commons Corridor into the Chamber, preceded by a Doorkeeper with the Serjeant-at-Arms bearing the Mace, and followed by his trainbearer, Chaplain and

The Speaker's Chair. The seats in front are for the Clerks of the House. The left-hand one is where the Chairman sits when the House goes into Committee.

Secretary. Before any business is conducted prayers are said as they have been since 1563 on every sitting day. The main prayer itself has remained unaltered since at least 1662 and the beauty and simplicity of the language make it fit to rank with anything in the Book of Common Prayer.

After prayers and the brief and formal dispatch of any private business (private bills promoted by local authorities or public bodies) the House moves, on every day other than Friday, to Question Time. Departments of State take it in turn to answer the questions and on Tuesdays and Thursdays the Prime Minister comes to the Dispatch Box and takes questions from 3.15 until 3.30 pm. After questions there may be ministerial statements, perhaps on business in the EEC or Government plans for a nationalized industry or on some major national or international event. These concluded, the House begins the main business of the day, perhaps a debate on the Second Reading of a Government Bill or on some general issue chosen by the Government or by the Opposition if it is one of their 'supply days'.

The Opposition parties have a right to a specified number of days during the parliamentary year when they can nominate the business irrespective of the wishes of the Government, and these days are still traditionally called 'supply days' as a reminder of the fact that the principal historic function of the House of Commons was the granting or witholding of 'supply' or revenue.

Just as the Opposition has the right to choose certain business, however embarrassing it might be to Government to have it discussed, so a number of days, normally Fridays, are set aside for the

discussion of bills and motions proposed by private Members who have been successful in one of the regular ballots held during the session. As a result of success in the ballots a number of important, and often controversial, pieces of social legislation which no Government has been inclined to embrace itself, have been allowed to reach the Statute Books: the Abolition of Capital Punishment and the Abortion Act are two prime examples.

When the House is in full session the Mace rests on the table of the House and Mr Speaker remains in control of the proceedings. Should the House go into Committee (and a number of major Bills are discussed by Committees of the whole House) the Mace rests under the table, Mr Speaker vacates the Chair and the Chairman of Ways and Means presides in one of the Clerk's chairs.

Normally the House adjourns at 10.30 pm on Mondays, Tuesdays, Wednesdays and Thursdays and at 3 pm on Fridays, the last half hour's business generally being a Motion for the adjournment, a procedure by which a private Member (again selected by ballot) has opportunity to draw attention to a subject of national or local concern for which time would otherwise not be found.

There are frequent occasions when this timetable is not followed and when the House sits late into the night, or right through it. Whenever the sitting finally ends the Speaker goes out of the Chamber through the door behind his Chair, preceded by the Mace, passing as he does so a large bag which hangs on the back of the Chair and into which Petitions presented by Members on behalf of their constituents are dropped before being conveyed to their appropriate destination, and ultimately stored in the Victoria Tower. The parliamentary day ends, whatever the time, with shouts of 'Who goes home?' and 'Usual time tomorrow' echoing through the Palace. These have rung out since the days when the streets around Westminster were so unsafe that parties of Members would go home together. And when there were no predetermined hours or strict timetables for parliament's meetings, Members had to be reminded of the time when the next day's business was to commence.

On either side of the Chamber are Division Lobbies, long rooms reminiscent of the galleries in Tudor houses. They are exactly similar, with long green benches running along the window side, an oriel window in the centre, and three tables where Members can attend to correspondence. The walls backing on to the Chamber are lined with copies of the official reports of parliamentary debates and bound copies of recent Statutes.

In the unreformed Parliament when the House divided one side went out of the Chamber and the other stayed in, the custom being that those who wanted to change the law went out in order to bring the new law in, while those whose vote was for maintaining the status quo remained seated.

Now, at the end of the debate, when the question is put by Mr Speaker, if it is contested, those in favour of the proposition troop into

Where the votes are cast. Exit from the 'Aye' Lobby.

One of the Division Lobbies in the Commons.

the 'Aye' lobby to the right of his Chair, those against go into the 'No' lobby. All over the Palace and in the adjacent offices, in Members' houses (and in certain restaurants) within a mile radius of the Palace, division bells ring. Members then have eight minutes to get themselves into the appropriate lobby before the doors are locked.

The entrance to the 'Aye' lobby is at the north end of the Chamber, that of the 'No' lobby at the south. This avoids the problem of having two groups of Members coming out of the lobbies simultaneously, having voted in opposite lobbies. In order to record his vote a Member gives his name to a Clerk who is seated at a high desk at the exit of the lobby, then he comes out, bowing to the two Tellers (one from each side) and is counted. At the end of the Division the Tellers, having given the figures to the Clerk of the House, line up in front of the table, bow to Mr Speaker and, the winning pair standing on the right, read out the figures.

Procedure in the Commons is rather more elaborate than that in the Lords. There there is no regular and full question time and Peers who desire to make a contribution to a debate merely signify their intentions knowing that they will be 'called'. Members of the Commons have no guarantee that they will have the chance to deliver their words of wisdom, however pregnant with speech they may be. It all depends on 'catching the Speaker's eye'.

If a Member wishes to speak he will generally write to the Speaker in advance, pressing his claim for consideration but he has no guarantee that, in seeking to ensure that all sides and opinions get a hearing, the Speaker will be able to call him. And so he sits in the Chamber and stands up in his place every time another Member finishes in the hope that he will hear his name called from the Chair. The Speaker is the only person who ever refers to a Member by name. All other Members refer to their colleagues by constituencies — 'The Honourable Member for . . .' or, if he is on your own side, 'My Honourable Friend the Member for . . .' If the Member referred to is a Queen's Counsel he is 'Honourable and Learned', if a Member of the Privy Council, 'The Right Honourable', and if he has held a commission in one of Her Majesty's forces, 'The Honourable and Gallant'. All this might seem rather formal and in strange contrast to the intimacy of the Chamber and the informality of its general structure. It does, however, prevent too much personal attack and abuse; indeed if a Member lets his tongue run away with him he may well be called to order for using 'un-parliamentary language'.

The physical structure of the Chamber derives from St Stephen's Chapel. When Edward VI gave members of his faithful Commons the Collegiate Chapel of St Stephen in which to hold their meetings, they moved into a building which had rows of stalls facing each other across a central aisle, and into a chapel which had at its east end an altar to which men bowed in reverence. Thus originated the seating structure of the Chamber and the custom of bowing to Mr Speaker's Chair.

St Stephen's Hall, looking towards the Central Lobby.

132

The visitor to the gallery of the present Commons has the chance to be reminded of this when he leaves through the Central Lobby for the main public exit from and entrance to the House. For leading out the Central Lobby he passes into St Stephen's Hall, so named because it was built on the site of the former Chamber. Its dimensions (95 feet long and 30 feet wide) are almost the same, and Barry's creation of this other great processional hall was a skilful answer to one of the constraints of the competition (how to incorporate Westminster Hall in his grand design) and also the challenge of how best to commemorate St Stephen's Chapel. He hit upon the happy expedient of throwing back the southern wall of Westminster Hall and inserting there a great window. This gave him the opportunity of creating a series of imposing steps, with a great platform in the midst on which so many great State occasions (including the presentation to the Queen of Loyal Addresses on the occasion of her Silver Jubilee) have taken place this century. The steps also afford a splendid view of the Hall.

St Stephen's Hall has a vaulted roof and large mosaic panels at either end; to the east is St Stephen, saint and martyr, with King Stephen on his right and King Edward the Confessor on his left, and to the west Edward III handing the design of the old St Stephen's Chapel to his master mason, Thomas of Canterbury.

Sir Thomas More, as Speaker of the House of Commons, confronts Cardinal Wolsey. One of the paintings from the 'Birth of Britain' series in St Stephen's Hall.

Statues in St Stephen's Hall. Fox faces Pitt almost on the spot where their great duels took place.

On either side of the Hall are nineteenth century statues of some of the more famous constitutional figures of the seventeenth and eighteenth centuries: Clarendon and Hampden, Walpole and Chatham, Pitt and Fox, Falkland (his spur broken by a suffragette who chained herself to it in 1908), Burke and Grattan, Selden and Mansfield.

Between the statues are eight large paintings, unveiled by Stanley Baldwin in 1927, depicting seminal events in the 'Building of Britain'. They are bold, graphic and arresting, if not great art. The subjects were decided by a Committee presided over by Sir Henry Newbolt, and care was taken not to enter into the realms of controversy by ensuring that the last subject chosen dated from early eighteenth century. It shows Queen Anne being presented with the Articles of Union by the English and Scottish Commissioners, prior to the Act of Union in 1707! Other panels show Alfred repulsing the Danes; Richard I setting off for the Crusades; John unwillingly assenting to Magna Carta; Wycliff's followers secretly reading his translation of the Bible; Sir Thomas More confronting Wolsey and, as Speaker of the House of Commons, refusing to grant supply without debate; Queen Elizabeth commissioning Raleigh to discover new lands; and Thomas Roe, James I's Ambassador at the court of the Mogul Emperor. Above the pictures are ten windows. All of them lost their glass during the blitz but they have been restored and the arms of Parliamentary cities and boroughs glow bright on a sunny day.

Beneath St Stephen's Hall is another relic of the ancient Palace, the

New Palace Yard. The entrance to Speaker's Court is on the left and that to Star Chamber Court in the centre.

The Crypt Chapel.

136

beautiful chapel of St Mary Undercroft. The 'Crypt Chapel', as it is generally known, has had a chequered history. It saw service as a cellar and as stables, and was used for many years as the Speaker's State Dining Rooms, his Chair being immediately beneath his Chair in the Chamber (the position of that and of the table of the House are marked by brass studs in the floor of St Stephen's Hall above).

The Crypt's restoration to religious use and full beauty is perhaps the greatest of Edward Barry's achievements. Realizing that here was one of the gems of medieval architecture, with its superb lierne vaulting (a pattern of non-structural ribs joining the main ones to form star-shaped and other patterns) he determined to make it one of the loveliest features of the Palace. It had escaped serious structural damage during the fire, although the stone was badly calcined and needed considerable attention and replacement. However, working in close association with Crace, he concentrated on doing this and on beautifying every inch of stonework with decoration in, so far as he could discover, the tones and colours of the original ornamentation. As it now stands, with its Minton tiled and marble floor, its fine stained glass windows by John Hardman, illustrating the life of St Stephen, and its superb original bosses which depict the martyrdoms of St Stephen, St John, St Catherine, St Laurence and St Margaret, beautifully picked out in gold and colour, it represents perhaps the greatest example of High Victorian Gothic art. Ayrton, the first Commissioner of Works, who dismissed Barry, reckoned it the 'most absolute waste of public money'.

Everything contributes to the overall effect. At the west are symbols of the Passion of Christ—the nails, the crown of thorns, the dice, the cock that crew. At the east of the altar are full-length figures of St Oswald, St Etheldreda, St Edmund, St Peter, St Margaret, St Stephen, St Edward the Confessor and St Edward the Martyr, and on the altar are two superb fifteenth century brass candlesticks. The altar rail and gates are replicas of the grille made in 1294 for the tomb of Eleanor of Castile in Westminster Abbey.

One of the glories of the Chapel is the octagonal baptistry with its incised representations of Noah and the Ark and of Moses holding the tablets of the law, and the lovely font of alabaster and marble.

In 1885 the Chapel escaped serious damage when a policeman discovered a large bomb placed there by the Fenians and bravely took it up to Westminster Hall where it exploded, shattering the great window and making a large hole in the floor. In 1911 Emily Davidson, one of the most militant of the suffragettes (she later committed suicide when she threw herself under the King's horse in the Derby) secreted herself in the Crypt in an attempt to escape the census of 1911. She was counted as a resident in the Palace.

Today the Crypt is used for regular celebrations of Holy Communion and Members of Parliament are allowed to have their children baptised and their daughters married there, or to be married there themselves.

It is a beautiful place in which to linger and to ponder on the history of the Palace before emerging again in the great Westminster Hall to marvel at Yevele's great roof, and the mastery with which Barry was able to incorporate this noblest of medieval halls into the most majestic of palaces.

CHAPTER SIX

The Palace of Westminster

THE WORKING PALACE

So much the visitor can see, but Barry's masterpiece does house over one thousand rooms, and it is still a working palace. The greater part of it, therefore, remains virtually unknown to those who do not have the privilege of serving there, and there are many Members of Parliament who make exciting discoveries after many years at Westminster, and many others who rarely pause to reflect on the beauties of a familiar environment.

There is no more familiar place to Members, and hardly anywhere more beautiful in the whole Palace than the cloisters of St Stephen's Chapel. John Chambre, the last Dean, paid for and supervised their construction between 1526 and 1529. They have something of the beauty of the exquisite Henry VII Chapel in the nearby Abbey and were doubtless worked on by some of the same masons. Two storeys high, the lower cloisters, like the Crypt, escaped the worst of the fire, though much of their stonework was badly scarred. Barry was determined to incorporate the cloisters in his design and great care was taken to ensure that they were meticulously restored, and where necessary, reproduced. The fine fan vaulting with its superb bosses of Tudor roses, portcullises, lilies and pomegranates received the most detailed attention, and the upper storey, which had been almost entirely destroyed, was faithfully recreated.

The most notable feature of the cloisters is the oratory on the west side. Tradition has it that here the death warrant of Charles I was signed, though in fact the Painted Chamber was almost certainly the place where most, if not all, of the regicides endorsed the fatal parchment.

The Oratory in the Cloisters, restored by Barry and now a Members' desk room. Here the Death Warrant of Charles I is reputed to have been signed.

Barry's renewed cloisters were again badly damaged by fire in 1941. Once more they were lovingly restored. Today the lower storey contains the private desks of many Members, while the upper, with the wide stone staircase which leads to it, is still the Members' main entrance to their lobby and the Chamber beyond.

In addition to the Chambers and the major lobbies and apartments through which the visitor passes the Principal Floor itself has a multitude of 'working' rooms. There is, for instance, the post office where Members and their secretaries collect their (normally vast) daily post, and behind the Speaker's Chair is the Table Office where they can hand in notices of questions which they wish to put to

Ministers. Here they can discuss their wording and that of Amendments and Motions with the Clerks who are always in attendance.

The Table Office is one of the five offices (the others are Public Bill Office, the Private Bill Office, the Committee Office and the Journal Office) which come under the jurisdiction of the Clerk of the House of Commons, who also has his apartments on this floor.

He is the most important official in the service of the House. He has a large staff of highly qualified Clerks responsible to him and his own office dates back to the fourteenth century. Until the seventeenth century his principal duty was to write the *Journals* of the House. As their importance as records of precedence and procedure grew, so did the importance of the Clerk's position, and by the eighteenth century he was recognized as the principal authority on Parliamentary rules and practice, turned to by successive Speakers whenever difficulties arose.

The Clerk who achieved the highest fame in this regard was the great Thomas Erskine May (later ennobled as Baron Farnborough). He was Clerk from 1871 until 1886 but it was in 1844, during his time as Assistant Librarian, a post he held from the age of sixteen (in 1831) that he produced his *Treatise on the Law, Privileges, Proceedings and Usage of Parliament* which, known simply as 'Erskine May', is still the 'Bible' of parliamentary procedure. Now in its nineteenth edition, it is consulted and quoted whenever disputes arise or judgements are given. Copies of it always lie on the table of the House and any Member of Parliament who wants to impress as a master of procedure claims it as his invariable bedside reading.

The Clerk, who is appointed by the Queen on the advice of the Prime Minister, and who will always have served in the Clerk's Department (the Deputy or Clerk Assistant is generally appointed to the post), is responsible for briefing the Speaker and available to advise Members on procedure and business. Every morning the Speaker has a meeting with him to discuss the day's business and to anticipate any troubles that might arise during debate, and when the House is sitting the Clerk must always be available to advise the Speaker. He spends many long hours at the Clerk's table immediately in front of the Speaker's chair and when he himself is not there two of his senior colleagues always are.

The Clerk's is not the only non-Member's chair always to be occupied when the House is sitting. Just below, and to the right of, the Bar of the House, facing Mr Speaker's Chair, sits the Serjeant-at-Arms (or one of his deputies), dressed in black court suit with knee breeches and buckle shoes, and a sword in a white scabbard. The Serjeant is privileged to carry the Mace of the House before the Speaker when he enters the Chamber each day and again when he leaves it, and on all ceremonial occasions. The Serjeant too is responsible for ensuring that the Speaker's orders respecting discipline of the House are carried out—hence the historic significance of the sword. In the nineteenth

The Speaker, Mr Selwyn Lloyd, leads the Commons to the Lords for the State Opening of Parliament, 1971.

century there were numerous occasions when Irish Members had to be carried struggling from the Chamber by the Serjeant and his assistants. Even today every year sees incidents when noisy strangers have to be ejected from the galleries.

To assist him in his duties the Serjeant has a number of doorkeepers and 'badge messengers'. Imposing men in full evening dress, with magnificent silver-gilt badges around their necks, they never fail to impress strangers. Like the Serjeant himself, who is always a senior retired officer, the doorkeepers and messengers almost invariably have distinguished service backgounds as regular non-commissioned officers.

The duties of the Serjeant-at-Arms extend far beyond the ceremonial and disciplinary. He is effectively 'in charge' of all the domestic arrangements for the House, and very many of the

employees who work in the precincts are responsible to him. This practice dates back to the House of Commons Offices Act of 1812. The Serjeant, too, comes into closer contact with the general public than any other senior official for he is in charge of all admissions to the public galleries.

At the other end of the Palace both Clerk and Serjeant have their counterparts. In the Lords there is a somewhat smaller body of Clerks, the senior of whom is the Clerk of the Parliaments, a title which, as we have noted, underlies the technical superiority of the Upper House. In the Lords the role of Serjeant-at-Arms was, in 1971, formally united with that of Black Rod.

The Gentleman Usher of the Black Rod, who summons the Commons to the Lords to listen to the speech from the throne and to hear various Royal Commissions, can trace his office back to 1348, and the foundation of the Order of the Garter.

Black Rod is the Usher of the Order and, in that capacity, still takes an active part in the Garter ceremony at Windsor. Like the Serjeant-at-Arms in the Commons, Black Rod has, since the mid-nineteenth century, always been a senior officer and, again like the Serjeant, has the responsibility for the administration of the House of Lords. He is answerable to the Lord Great Chamberlain for the maintenance of the

Royal apartments.

Black Rod's role is, however, as befits the House he serves, a more colourful one than the Serjeant's. He has charge of all the administrative arrangements for the State Opening of Parliament, and he leads the procession whenever a new Peer, resplendent in his (generally hired) finery takes his seat in the House. When he goes to summon the Commons to hear the speech from the throne the door is firmly shut, although the House of Commons has no power to refuse him admission when he has knocked the ritual thrice on their door.

Black Rod's has always been a coveted position, and in the earlier days it was actively and eagerly sought after because of the perquisites which went with it. In the seventeenth century and eighteenth century, for instance, he not only received fees from any delinquents imprisoned by him on behalf of the House of Lords but could also levy fees from Lords who were taking their seats. These fees ranged from £2.10s for a Baron to £10.00 for a Duke, and, together with those he received from the numerous Bills that were promoted in the House of Lords, that meant that his salary, nominally a little over £300 per year, often exceeded £3,000. In addition he had a profitable sideline in the sale of offices. There were many anxious to serve in the Lords as doorkeepers and housemaids, and other ostensibly menial roles, because those posts too carried with them the opportunity of attractive additional fees.

Both Black Rod and the Serjeant-at-Arms have offices on, or just off, the Principal Floor, and on this floor too a number of senior Ministers have rather splendid apartments. The most magnificent is the Prime Minister's room which still contains some of the finest furniture Pugin designed for the Palace. A particularly attractive feature of almost all the main ministerial rooms is the collection of drawings, watercolours and prints they contain. These and the others scattered about the whole building provide a fascinating pictorial history of the Palace, and constitute what is possibly the most comprehensive collection of Parliamentary pictures in the world. Many of them have been given by former Members or Peers but a number have been acquired in recent years by the Department of the Environment and by the Speaker's Art Fund—a fund made up from profits from the sale of literature within the Palace and of Christmas cards to Members.

The Lords has fewer imposing Ministerial rooms but it does have a magnificent Committee Room on the Principal Floor, the Moses Room, so called after the large fresco of Moses bringing down the tablets of the law, painted by J. R. Herbert in 1864. Like the other frescoes it has faded somewhat, a fate which has not overtaken Herbert's other picture in the same room, 'The Judgement of Daniel', an oil painting on canvas. The Moses Room is frequently used by the Law Lords to hear Appeals, and by the Ecclesiastical Committee, one of the few Committees composed of Members of both Houses, generally meets here to discuss the legislation of the Church of England before it is presented to Parliament.

The Moses Room in the House of Lords.

It is difficult to imagine a modern legislator, serving on the Ecclesiastical Committee or anywhere else, being able to begin to discharge his functions without the supporting facilities which only the best of libraries can provide. However, before the nineteenth century neither the Lords nor Commons possessed a library. The need was not so great in an age when every Member had his handsomely furnished town house, and when Parliament met less frequently and churned out less laws, but by 1818 Members of the Commons had come to the conclusion that their small library, containing only the journals of the House and official papers, established in 1800, was insufficient, and so in that year a room 17 feet square was provided within the Palace and a Librarian appointed. By 1834 there were three rooms and an annual expenditure of £2,000 on books but the rooms and two-thirds of their contents were destroyed in the fire. The Lords fared slightly better. Though the single room which Soane had converted for them in 1826 was totally destroyed almost all of the books were saved. They were among the papers passed along the line of soldiers and stacked in St Margaret's.

Barry was instructed to include adequate library facilities for both Houses in the new Palace. He rose to the challenge. On the river front, away from the bustle of the Principal Floors, and with one of the finest views in London, a series of splendid rooms was constructed and on them Pugin lavished loving care. The Lords had four spacious, light and airy rooms, and the Commons five (a sixth room was annexed from the Speaker's residence in 1966).

Both libraries are extremely well stocked and their staffs provide an excellent research service. No query is too mundane or too esoteric to meet with a prompt and courteous statement of the obvious or analysis of the profound. A very wide range of newspapers and periodicals is taken and stored, and there is a comprehensive foreign service as well. One of the rooms in the Commons library now houses a computer terminal which can provide instant information from a number of data banks.

A corner of the Library in the House of Commons.

The river front of the Principal Floor provides facilities for more than intellectual refreshment. The first half of the nineteenth century was the great age of the London Clubs and the Members of the reformed Parliament were determined (for all their minute scrutiny of the accounts and ostentatious consciousness of public expenditure) that their own House should not provide inferior facilities to those they could enjoy a mile away. As Alexander Beresford Hope, the Tory Member for Maidstone, remarked, 'The House of Commons ought to be the best club in the world'. He and many of his colleagues were not entirely satisfied with the result of Barry's endeavours to make it so. They complained of 'the most scanty and grudging accommodation', alleging that 'the libraries were too large and the dining rooms too small'.

That there were dining rooms at all would have been an agreeable surprise to the ghost of any earlier Parliamentarian. We have a

number of entertaining accounts of Members munching in the Chamber in the seventeenth and eighteenth centuries and it was not until 1773 that any food could be purchased within the precincts of the Palace. Before that Members had to repair to one of the Coffee Houses or taverns clustered around. In days when the main meal of the day was taken in the early afternoon (at the latest) and when Parliament, to accommodate this habit, met from eight o'clock in the morning until noon* there was neither the need for, nor the opportunity of taking, a full dinner at Westminster. But habits changed and sittings extended and as a result those Members who lived particularly close to the Palace regularly entertained their colleagues. Wilberforce was one. He seems to have kept open house: 'It delighted us to see our friends in this way, particularly as it gave us the opportunity of talking upon any important points of public business without any great sacrifice of time. Those who came up late put up with a mutton chop or beef steak. The Duke of Montrose called

*At the beginning of the seventeenth century the House met at 6 am.

in one day as we were thus employed and declined taking anything. Seeing, however, so many around him busy with knife and fork he said, "I cannot resist any longer" and sat down to a mutton chop.'

In 1773 John Bellamy was appointed Deputy Housekeeper in the Palace and, enterprising man that he was, began to provide food for Members. Whether the Young Pitt did in fact call for 'one of Bellamy's meat pies' with his dying words in 1806 is doubtful but by the early nineteenth century Bellamy's was well established and some Members seem to have passed rather more time there than in the Chamber. Dickens gives us an amusing description of the place in *Sketches by Boz*. He describes one of the regulars as 'a very old frequenter of Bellamy's, much addicted to stopping "after the House is up . . ." and a complete walking reservoir of spirits and water . . . Members arrive every moment in a great bustle to report that "the Chancellor of the Exchequer is up" and to get great glasses of brandy and water to sustain them during a division.' Even then, however, there were adverse comments about the catering, a Bellamy's sandwich being defined as 'two small slices of bread and butter, almost transparent, with a stale slice of thin ham or beef between them . . . Bellamy charges one shilling for them and they don't stand him above twopence.' To be fair, however, both to Bellamy and to Pitt, we do learn that five shillings and six pence 'secured the most expensive dinner that could be had; steaks, veal pie, mutton chops to any extent, with tarts, salads, pickles, toasted cheese, etc.' The Bellamys, father and son, fed legislators for sixty years until the fire swept their rooms away. Barry had then to provide proper dining facilities for a legislature that was increasingly given to sitting long hours, even if it was civilized enough to adjourn for dinner—a practice that continued well into this century.

Though some had criticized both the rooms and the food, we learn that at the beginning of this century a staff of twenty cooks was employed and that one hundred and eleven thousand meals were served during a session which lasted barely six months. Then, 'for a modest shilling' the frugal Member could 'obtain a meal adequate for his simple needs. An inclusive charge of two shillings secures a plain dinner of three courses. An additional shilling commands a more elaborate meal; while if a Member spends five shillings he can fare most sumptuously on all the delicacies in season. The wine list is framed on lines as comprehensive as those of the bill of fare. A bottle of excellent claret costs no more than ten pence and a bottle of light hock or Graves may be obtained for a shilling. These charges are indicative of the principles on which "the best Club in London" is worked.'

Today the Lords have a large dining room on the Principal Floor and a Guest Room where they can entertain friends for drinks on the river front. The Members' Dining Room of the Commons is also on the river front and next to it is the Strangers' Dining Room in which Members can entertain guests. Each room has a number of interesting Parliamentary pictures. There are portraits of the Younger Pitt, Speaker Onslow, Gladstone, Walpole and Disraeli in the Members' Dining Room, while in the Strangers' are Cromwell, John Pym and Speaker Lenthall. Perhaps the most exciting feature of these two rooms however, is the magnificent Pugin wallpaper, recently reprinted from the original blocks and bringing back the bold splash of Gothic colour and ornamentation which their designer envisaged.

Between the Members' Dining Room and the library is the Chess Room (where Members can indulge in the only indoor game which is officially allowed within the precincts) and the Members' Smoking Room. Barry provided a Lower Smoking Room which opened onto the Terrace and where Members could take their guests. From the old prints we have it does not look particularly comfortable. It had a tiled floor and partially tiled walls, so that the smell of tobacco would not be retained by the furnishings.

Today's Smoking Room (Barry's Members' Smoking Room) is much more comfortable, with deep leather chesterfields and armchairs, and is panelled and carpeted throughout. This Smoking Room is very much the 'holy of holies'. Only Members (or Members of the Lords who were formerly Members of the Commons) are allowed to cross its threshold. In this it is unique, for the Members' Dining Room has a table for the Clerks of the House and they, and other officials, are

The Members' Dining Room in the Commons.

The Members' Smoking Room in the Commons.

allowed to use part of the Members' Tearoom.

There are a number of bars where visitors can be entertained in both Houses. On the Terrace Floor for instance in addition to two cafeterias, there is a bar known affectionately as 'The Kremlin'. Here and in Annie's Bar (named after a former barmaid), where press and politicians meet, no licensing hours are enforced and sounds of revelry can be heard by day as well as by night.

Also on the Terrace floor are a series of small dining rooms which can be booked by Members for private functions. They are much in demand, especially during the winter months, and by those Members who have constituencies in London and the Home Counties. At the southern end of the Commons Terrace corridor is a Grill Room (Barry's Lower Smoking Room) known as the Harcourt Room after Lewis Harcourt who was made first Commissioner of Works in 1907. Here is a collection of Nash prints of the Great Exhibition and a sunny painting of Venice by Churchill, given by his widow.

On either side of the staircase leading from the Principal Floor to the Terrace are Professor Ernest Tristram's re-creations of the medieval wall paintings from the Painted Chamber and St Stephen's Chapel. Although they inevitably lack the spontaneity of the originals they do give a vivid idea of the beauties that were lost in the great fire, for very detailed copies of the paintings had been made in the early years of the nineteenth century and it was from these that Tristram worked so painstakingly some sixty years ago.

In the Lobby by the doors which give on to the Terrace is the original hammer of Big Ben—the one that caused all the trouble when the bell was first cracked—while further along the Terrace corridor is a glass case containing reminders of the greatest trouble of all—a series of tally sticks, such as caused the fire in 1834. In another case is one of the original annunciators first installed in 1895 in various parts of the building to indicate on long, wide and loudly clacking tape, the name of the speaker in the Chamber at that moment. In 1968 these machines were replaced in the Commons by closed circuit television annunciators and a similar system was installed in the House of Lords in 1973.

Wherever one goes in the Palace one cannot escape from reminders of its history. Some of the finest watercolours, and the most accurate records, of the destroyed Palace hang in this dingy Terrace corridor where they are rarely seen, and even more rarely appreciated.

Behind the Terrace corridor the basement is a veritable warren of rooms. Apart from a large suite of modern kitchens, there are innumerable storerooms and the offices of the Refreshment Department. Beneath the Chamber there are more Ministers' rooms and conference rooms, and a Transport Office where Members can book tickets for Bognor or Bangkok. There are boiler rooms, and under the Central Lobby is a vault which was equipped with machine tools during the Second World War and where a team of workers, Members, officials and others made precision instruments for the Ministry of Supply. There is even a shooting range where Members

Two of Professor Tristram's reconstructions of the medieval wall paintings formerly in St Stephen's Chapel.

The Water Gate entrance to New Palace Yard, c. 1800.

and staff can practice their marksmanship. In 1964 the Labour Member for West Lothian, Tam Dalyell, hunting for rooms which could be converted to Members' use, discovered a blacksmith's forge and 'In an area of 590 square feet, a man pressing his trousers.' Since then a number of adjustments and alterations have been made but the cellars and basement of the House still have an air of mystery about them which makes the annual search on the eve of the Opening of Parliament (to commemorate Gunpowder Plot) by a Company of Yeomen of the Guard more than just quaintly charming.

Above the stairs which lead to the Terrace is the Lower Waiting Hall. Its chief use is as a thoroughfare for Members to the dining rooms and the Smoking Room, library and Speaker's office, but there is a splendid chimney piece around which Members frequently sit to interview constituents who have descended upon them in the Central Lobby, and, by the corridor leading to the dining room, a rugged bust of Keir Hardy. The Hall also contains the Book of Remembrance in which are inscribed the names of Members and servants of the House, and the sons and daughters of Members, who were killed during the Second World War. A relatively recent innovation is the Families Room which leads off this Hall and in which Members' families are allowed to wait while the business of the nation is dispatched.

It is at the foot of the Grand Staircase leading to the Upper Waiting Hall that Barry has his undeservedly hidden memorial, a sensitive larger than life statue by J. H. Folly which shows the architect poring over the designs of his masterpiece. Up the stairway are busts of the Younger Pitt, the assassinated Prime Minister, Spencer Perceval, Canning, Peel, Palmerston and Gladstone, whilst on the landing is the most unmemorable and unsuccessful essay in historical narrative painting in the Palace: a picture by Solomon J. Solomon of Queen Elizabeth being petitioned to marry by the Commons. With delusions of Renaissance grandeur the artist has included portraits of some of the celebrities of his day, Speaker Lowther, John Burns, Lewis Harcourt, and Lord Swaythling, who had the misfortune of having to pay for the ghastly thing.

As always in the Palace, it pays to look up in ascending these stairs. For there hang the beautiful brass chandeliers which hung in the Court of Requests and which therefore lit the temporary Chamber of the Commons until the completion of Barry's Chamber.

The Upper Waiting Hall, onto which the stairs open, was known as the Poets' Hall because the walls were originally decorated with a series of frescoes illustrating English poetry. Episodes from Chaucer, Byron, Spenser, Milton, Dryden, Scott and, of course, Shakespeare (Lear disinheriting Cordelia) greeted the visitor—but not for long. Within a decade they were in a parlous state. One Member remarked that they were coming off the walls and he thought it would be a good thing if they did. Although his sentiments were not universally shared, every attempt to arrest the disintegration failed and all are now covered over, though their titles can still be discerned carved on

Committee Room 14 in the Commons. Seamore's picture of the flight of the Five Members is on the wall. In this committee room the Conservative Party's 1922 Committee of all its Back Benchers meets every week when the House is in session.

the sills beneath.

The most notable feature of the Upper Waiting Room is the superb mahogany table of the House which stood in the Commons from about 1730 until 1800 when it was moved to the cloisters. It was the finest piece of furniture rescued from the fire. Disraeli is here too in the form of a life-size statue by Count Gleichen, looking quizically towards the machine where indifferent tea and appalling coffee are dispensed into paper cups at the press of a switch. The machine is there to sustain Members, for this is the Committee Floor. Stretching out from either side of the Upper Waiting Hall is a long corridor, flanked on the river side by sixteen Committee Rooms of varying sizes. The smaller ones are used for meetings of Select Committees, the larger for Standing Committees discussing Bills before the House.

The size of these Committees varies according to the importance of the legislation, and is always related proportionally to the strength of the parties in the House of Commons. In the Committees the Members sit behind tables but face each other as in the Chamber. Each Committee is presided over by one of the Members of the Panel of Chairmen who, for the duration of the Committee stage of the Bill in question, witholds his Party allegiance and votes and behaves as Mr Speaker would do in the Chamber below.

Most of the Committee Rooms are furnished as Pugin originally designed them, and a number have, like the dining room below, recently been re-papered according to his scheme. They contain a number of the more notable of Westminster's pictures. In Committee Room 10 for instance is G. F. Watts picture of 'Alfred exciting the Saxons to repel the Danes' and Frank Salisbury's 'Burial of the Unknown Warrior' while in Number 11 is an interesting (historically speaking) picture by Lawson of the Speaker's Procession in 1884. The most dramatic is Seamore's account of 'The Flight of the Five Members' in Number 14, the largest and best adorned of all the Committee Rooms. This has been the scene of many dramatic and stormy Party meetings. Here every Thursday when the House is in session the Conservative backbenchers of the '1922 Committee' foregather and it was here that the ballots which led to Mrs Thatcher's election as leader of the Party took place.

At the southern end of the corridor, which is lined with a series of portraits of major Parliamentarians on loan from the National Portrait Gallery, are two modern Committee Rooms and there are also six Committee Rooms for the House of Lords. These do not complete the Palace's Committee facilities. The larges Committee room of all is the Grand Committee Room adjoining Westminster Hall. This was the room that was wrecked by the I.R.A. bomb in 1974 and which has since been restored to more than its former glory. Here Cecil Rhodes and Dr Jameson gave evidence before a Select Committee of the House in 1897 and here meetings are held whenever a major international or national figure, such as the Secretary-General of the United Nations, addresses Members of the House. It is also equipped with facilities for showing films.

All meetings of Standing Committees, and most meetings of Select Committees, are open to the public and even the smallest have some seats available for those who wish to come and listen. Committee work is an aspect of Parliamentary activity that receives little publicity but Members can often be seen at their least flamboyant and forensic best in the detailed examination of witnesses before a Select Committee, or in the minute consideration of the Clauses of a Bill.

Committee Rooms are also much in demand by Party and All Party Committees. Both of the major parties have Committees covering every Departmental subject, where Ministers or Shadow Ministers are grilled, and non-parliamentary experts invited to address Members. In recent years the All Party Committees have also increased in number and importance and on every day of the week, save Friday, there are upwards of a dozen Committee meetings of one sort or another between the hours of four and six.

Above the Committee Corridor, and on the third storey of the Palace, is the Upper Committee Corridor where a number of Members, including the Chairmen of important Committees, have their rooms. In 1979 the Select Committee structure was altered and twelve new Committees were appointed to Shadow Government Departments. A

Giants of the nineteenth century: top left *George Canning, a painting by Sir Thomas Lawrence;* bottom left *Mr Gladstone, a painting by Sir John Millais;* top right *Benjamin Disraeli, also by Millais;* bottom right *Lord Randolph Churchill, a cartoon by Phil May.*

number of rooms for these new Select 'Subject' Committees were opened in this corridor in 1980. Here too are a series of television rooms where Members can watch the various television channels or see video-recordings of important broadcasts they missed on their original transmission. It is a quiet reach of the building with views over the Thames that were no doubt enchanting in Barry's day but are now marred by such sights as the new and grotesque St Thomas's Hospital across the river.

On these two Committee floors are the Committee Offices and the Public and Private Bill Offices, all manned by Clerks. Sometimes a Member will sleep all night outside the Public Bill Office in order to register his name for a Ten Minute Rule Bill. On most Tuesdays and Wednesdays a Member is able to seek leave to introduce a Bill under the 'Ten Minute Rule'. This means that he can make a speech of approximately ten minutes in which he can advocate some new piece of legislation. The chances of its ever getting on the Statute Book are remote but it gives him a chance to ride a hobby horse and is therefore for him, although not necessarily for the rest of the House, often anxious to move to the next business, a splendid opportunity. Hence the popularity of the procedure and the willingness of some Members to take up station for an uncomfortable night in order to be first in the queue. A successful Member knows that his efforts will, if not remembered by posterity, at least be noticed by the gentlemen who occupy the northern end of the building: the Press.*

For several centuries there were no detailed reports of parliamentary proceedings. The Clerks of the Parliaments had entered details of Petitions and Bills on the Parliament Rolls since the end of the thirteenth century and by the turn of the fifteenth the Clerks in both Houses sometimes made brief records of debates. Only one or two of these, and notes of speeches in their 'scribbled books' and manuscript minutes of the seventeenth century, survive. Neither Lords nor Commons would allow these to be published, and indeed the Commons resolved in 1628 that 'entry by the Clerk of particular men's speeches was without warrant at all times'. We are singularly fortunate therefore to have Rushworth's detailed record of Charles I's descent upon Parliament to arrest the five Members in January, 1642.

From the brief laconic records in the *Journals* of the House, as from surviving diaries of Members, we get something of the flavour of events and debates, though brevity is the hallmark of many of the more significant entries in the *Journal.* Thus for 5 November, 1605, it reports, 'This last night the Upper House of Parliament was searched by Sir Thos. Knevett; and one Johnson, a servant to Mr Thomas Percy, was there apprehended; who had placed thirty-six barrels of gun powder in the vault under the House with a purpose to blow up the King, and the whole Company, when they should there assemble.

*Though the present system did not apply, 300 bills were presented by Private Members in 1901. Then, as now, Members were anxious to 'prove their usefulness', as a contemporary writer has it.

Afterwards divers other gentlemen were discovered to be of the plot.'

We know too that seventeenth-century Members, like some of their successors, did not always act with the dignity their office should demand. Pepys, on 29 December, 1666 reports 'how Sir Alan Broderick and Alan Aspley did come drunk the other day into the House and did both speak for half an hour together, and could not be laughed, or pulled, or bid sit down and hold their peace, to the great contempt of the King's servants and cause; which I am grieved at with all my heart.'

Anchitell Grey, Member for Derby for almost thirty years at the end of the seventeenth century, wrote a voluminous account of debates in the House during his period. It is full of delightful anecdotes, as when he records in February, 1677, 'There was great silence for sometime. Mr. Williamson: whilst we sit still and say nothing you must do something in the Chair or we shall do nothing. Mr Powle: I wonder not at the silence of the Committee if every man is in the dark as well as I.' Mr Powle was later voted into the Chair by the Convention Parliament of 1689 and quickly became a trusted advisor of William III, who made him Master of the Rolls.

Even the unreformed Parliament was conscious of electoral popularity. No doubt this is why, in March, 1776, when a tax on dogs was proposed the *Journal* reports, 'Motion deferring consideration "four months" was carried.'

The cost of living obviously concerned Members too and thus the *Journal* for 1 May, 1768: 'Mr Heath said that he attends Smithfield Market: that he has formerly bought there veal for $2\frac{1}{2}$ and 3 pence per pound and the price is now 5 pence per pound.' And again in 1787 a Petition of the Lord Mayor and citizens of London urged 'That the great advance in the price of meat and other provisions of late years are distressing the middle and lower classes of people, has a tendency immediately to injure and at length to destroy the manufacturers and commerce of the Kingdom.'

During the eighteenth century more and more attempts were made to report events to an increasingly interested public—mainly those who took the numerous magazines and journals that circulated in the coffee houses of the Capital. Twice the House declared publication of its debates to be a breach of privilege but the practice continued, and during the last quarter of the century was openly tolerated. Dr Johnson was one of those who was particularly prolific in composing, often from somewhat garbled and dubious accounts, reports of proceedings in the House. In 1801 some of the accumulated records of debates were published by William Cobbett under the title of 'Parliamentary History', and in 1803 the press were given a special reserved portion of the gallery. Cobbett himself was responsible for reporting debates until 1812 and many Members feel it rather unfair that Hansard's name and not his should be immortally associated with the Official Report.

However, the task of publishing it was entrusted to Thomas

Hansard and he and his son were responsible for the reports until 1892. These were not, as we have them, entirely verbatim. Hansard and the later outside contractors who had the responsibility for printing them were, until 1908, allowed to cut backbenchers' speeches by up to two-thirds. In that year the House decided that it would have its own staff of reporters and that there would be no discrimination between the reporting of Ministers' and Members' speeches. And so from 1909 the Official Report has been a verbatim record of the proceedings and each morning, providing no industrial action has interrupted its even flow, Members of both houses can have on their breakfast tables reports of the previous day's proceedings up to 10 pm.

There are fourteen Parliamentary reporters who take turns in taking shorthand notes and then dictating to a typist. The Editorial staff of *Hansard* then checks the typed script and the Member himself, or the Minister's representative, is allowed to read it through to ensure that it is accurate, although he is not allowed to make any alterations that would change the meaning of his words.

The proceedings of Standing Committees are similarly reported, though here there is considerable reliance on tape-recording machines. Reports of Select Committees, however, are still in the hands of a private firm, successor to that established by Joseph Gurney who reported the trial of Warren Hastings and whose son was made the first official shorthand writer to both Houses in 1813 an appointment which is still held by the senior partner of the firm.

In Barry's Chamber provision was made in the galleries for reporters and when the Commons Chamber was rebuilt this was extended. All national, and most major provincial, papers have their parliamentary correspondents, as do the principal press agencies and the radio and television networks. They follow in the steps of many a distinguished journalist, including Charles Dickens, who began his writing career reporting parliamentary debates when he was only twenty.

Dickens and his colleagues, however, would have marvelled at the extra facilities that today's reporters enjoy. The *Hansard* staff have a series of rooms devoted to their use, *The Times* has its own room and many Members envy the conditions in which the press operate. They have their own catering facilities and the special Press Gallery lunches, at which leading politicians are invited to speak, are among the parliamentary occasions for which invitations are most welcome.

One of the more notable features of these lunches, and indeed of the general atmosphere prevailing in the gallery and the lobby, is the friendly relationship between politicians and journalists. Though there are inevitably moments of tension and conflicts of interest these are rare and there are many firm and fast friendships of long years standing between those who sit in the gallery and frequent the lobbies, and the politicians whose speeches and actions provide a basis for their reports and speculations.

Charles Dickens, perhaps the most famous Parliamentary reporter of all time.

The press are not the only ones to have demanded, and been given, more space in recent years. Barry's Palace has proved to be infinitely adaptable, and as the role of the Member of Parliament has changed, and as Governments have increased in numbers (today a Government consists of a hundred or more Ministers ranging from the Prime Minister to the most junior Minister or Assistant Whip) so the demands for extra rooms and facilities has had to be answered. Unfortunately the answers have not always shown that appreciation of the beauties of a very great building which the more sensitive would have wished. There has been infilling within the Star Chamber (so called because it was on the site of the old Star Chamber which earned such notoriety in Tudor and Stuart times) and there was even a wooden hut erected on the roof to provide extra accommodation for *Hansard* reporters.

It was during the 1960's that the demands for better and more individual accommodation for Members, and for the increased numbers of staff, grew more vociferous. Some of the debates would have been incomprehensible to parliamentarians of an earlier generation. Early in this century, for instance, a commentator waxed eloquent on 'the comparatively modern innovation' of a room set apart for secretarial work, where 'busy Members contrive in the intervals of their legislative labours, to transact, with the aid of private secretaries, a considerable amount of urgent work, both connected with their parliamentary duties and their private business. Type-writers are available in the building, and the telephone is also at hand so that it is possible for an active legislator to make the utmost use of his leisure'.

This happy state lasted for many years. As late as 1930, according to Sir Barnett Cocks, who retired as Clerk to the House (after serving forty-three years there) in 1973: 'There were perhaps two typewriters in the House of Commons. The most literate of officials, the Clerk of the House, kept incoming letters unfiled in a black box, as his predecessors had done as far back as the Long Parliament of Charles I's reign . . . It was not until 1932 that the first solitary young woman typist, an almost anonymous Miss Smith, was engaged to work on the staff of the House of Commons. A year earlier the first steel filing cabinet was introduced to hold the handful of letters which were kept from those days.'

Even during the numerous 'space debates' of the 1960's, there were those Members who vehemently opposed any change in facilities and who saw no need for improvement. One of these was Michael Clark Hutchinson, who had entered the House as Conservative Member for an Edinburgh constituency as late as 1957. He did not want 'any change whatsoever. In fact I am delighted with the House and the Palace of Westminster. I have never found the accommodation too small or too overcrowded . . . I do not want a telephone. I detest that instrument enough already and I shall certainly take what steps I can to prevent one being foisted on me . . . In my view a lot of this

Norman Shaw's great building on the Embankment, formerly Scotland Yard, now houses the offices of some 200 Members of Parliament.

157

"fussation" about accommodation is an agitation from those on the Left Wing. They want to put their fingers in the till and inflate themselves at public expense.'

However, his Scottish Labour colleague, the anti-monarchist Willie Hamilton, spoke, in this at least, for more Members when he delivered a scathing attack on the facilities Members had to endure. When he had come to the House in 1950 he had been given a key to a locker no bigger than the one he had had at school. It was the only accommodation he had in the building. Twelve years later things were rather better. 'I now have a little desk upstairs, right at the top. I go up in an old antiquated lift and I eventually get right to the top of the building. I am with another seven Members in a room the size of an average dining room in the average Council house. All the time, every day in midsummer, we have to have artificial light. I sit furthest away from a very narrow window and I must put on the lights on an August day like today. The room is ideal for a suicide. If I could squeeze out of the window I could throw myself, and sometimes feel like doing so, into the Thames.'

Apart from the in-filling mentioned (which has had unhappily distorting effects upon Barry's architecture) grand schemes were proposed. New Palace Yard was to be enclosed, if not as Barry had quite intended, at least in a style sympathetic to his structure. The scheme was abandoned.

The Speaker's Drawing Room.

It was then proposed to erect a vast new Parliamentary complex across the road in Bridge Street. A competition was held and the winning design, which called for a huge building covered in sheets of tinted glass providing Members not only with rooms, rest rooms and restaurants, but with a roof garden and sauna baths, was approved and then, in the aftermath of the economic crisis of 1973, abandoned—much to the relief of those who felt that such a structure would have been glaringly incongruous in the context of Parliament Square.

Members, however, do not now have to dictate all their letters in corridors or in odd corners perched on uncomfortable benches. The old headquarters of the Metropolitan Police, the two splendid buildings designed by the Victorian architect, Norman Shaw, on the Embankment, have now been given over to Members and many have, at worst, to share a room with no more than a couple of colleagues, even if they have the inconvenience of a five minute walk to the Chamber. There is even a gymnasium, with sauna, for the fitness fiends. Within the precincts of the Palace itself the only major modern addition has been the underground car park which cost more than the original Palace to construct and which certainly rendered prophetic the words of that early twentieth-century admirer of the new secretarial facilities who had written, 'a further concession to the spirit of progress that has been made in late years is the provision along the side of the Star Chamber Court of a convenient place for the storage of bicycles . . . Special accommodation for motors has yet to be

158

The entrance to the Speaker's House in Speaker's Court.

The Speaker's Dining Room.

supplied but doubtless it will be forthcoming in the not too distant future.'

One of the problems confronting those who saw the need for extra accommodation which the changing role of the Member, and the longer sittings of Parliament, made necessary, was the number of residences within the Palace. Barry's Houses provided for no less than sixteen of these, many of them grandly proportioned. The Lord Chancellor had fifty-six rooms at his disposal, twenty-nine of them in his private residence. (He still has forty for his legal staff.) The Serjeant-at-Arms had forty rooms. 'Dammit, a fella has to live somewhere', as one of the occupants of that office remarked when it was suggested that he might give up the odd drawing-room or two.

Today much more modest facilities are provided for those who have to live on the premises. The Serjeant-at-Arms has a pleasant, but none too large, flat, having given up a whole suite of rooms and placed them at the disposal of the Leader of the Opposition and Shadow Cabinet. As befits his office the Lord Chancellor still has spacious rooms in the southern tower on the river front of the building, while in the northern tower on the same front is Mr Speaker's official residence. No Member of Parliament would begrudge him his apartments for they are, in a very real sense, part of the House. Today the Speaker lives in what the late Lord Selwyn Lloyd, Speaker from 1971 to 1976, described as 'one of the most delightful flats in London', on the top

159

floor of the residence. That he has to be 'above the shop' nobody would dispute for he is constantly on call to preside at meetings, discuss problems, see officials and Members, even when the House itself is not sitting or he is not in the Chair—and he frequently does duty there until well past midnight.

The State Rooms, in which previous Speakers used to live in great style, are now wholly reserved for official entertaining of Members and distinguished visitors, and when the Speaker does receive visitors from home or overseas it is always in a parliamentary context.

Though things are still done in Speaker's House with great dignity there has been some alteration in style. At the beginning of the century when, as we are told, 'to receive an invitation to a Speaker's Reception' was a cherished ambition of every young Member . . . 'For social recognition is to the budding legislator what presentation at Court is to the aspiring young damsel', Members were expected to observe, 'immutable regulations, sumptuary or otherwise, for these entertainments. Uniform or court dress is indispensable' . . . or almost always: 'During the Short Parliament of 1885 when there were a dozen Labour Members in the House, and they were sufficient in themselves to form a dinner party, the late Speaker (Lord Peel) with characteristic kindness of heart asked them in a body to dine with him and to wear whatever costume they pleased.'

Just as customs and costumes have changed so have the State Rooms. They, like the other residences within the Palace, were originally fully furnished with pieces designed or inspired by Pugin. But today only the State Dining Room remains virtually unaltered, and in that the decoration, though Puginesque in character, dates from some six years after his death. However, it is one of the most splendid apartments in the whole Palace with its superb chimneypiece, seating for thirty-six people, and portraits of former Speakers around the walls. The other State Rooms, drawing-rooms and the study (The Speaker's Library was absorbed into the Commons in 1966) contain some of the original furniture and all have great charm and beauty. Alas, however, the most fascinating piece of furniture of all, the State bed, is gone. It was rediscovered in 1978 in a Welsh farmhouse, having been bought at a sale some thirty years ago. It is a magnificent affair—'a walnut and gilt Arabian bedstead, 7' 6″ by 6' 6″, with ornamental carved decorations'.

The first Speaker to live in the Palace of Westminster was Henry Addington (1789–1801) and his portrait has pride of place at the top of the Grand Staircase which leads from the official entrance to the residence in Speaker's Court. It was Addington who began that collection of Speaker's portraits (which forms a unique record of many of the occupants of the office) most of which were fortunately rescued during the great fire.

The portraits do not go back as far as the first Speaker. The first recorded holder of the actual title was Sir Thomas Hungerford in 1377 and for a period of well over one hundred years each Parliament

Roof bosses in the Crypt Chapel.

elected a different Speaker, or Spokesman, at its first meeting. He was elected at the King's command and his duty was to act as the spokesman of the Commons in the royal presence. Between 1377 and 1523, when Sir Thomas More became Speaker for a brief period, no less than fifty-seven men held the office, a number of them on two or three separate occasions. Two of the earliest Speakers, Sir James Pickering and Sir John Goldsborough in 1378 and 1379 respectively, attempted to assert the right of the Commons before their Sovereign, and incurred the royal displeasure as a result. It was hardly surprising, therefore, that the honour of being elected was neither eagerly sought nor warmly welcomed. As early as 1381 Sir Richard Waldegrave physically demonstrated his reluctance to take the Chair, and so began a tradition that is re-enacted to this day whenever a new Speaker is elected, and his proposer and seconder take him and instal him in the Chair, after he has displayed an ostensible unwillingness to sit there.

Sometimes more than mere Royal displeasure was incurred. When Henry IV came to the throne he had Speaker Bussy beheaded. He was not the last Speaker to find himself in trouble in those turbulent times and it is small wonder that some Speakers adopted a tone of particular obsequiousness when talking to the King. Even Thomas More felt obliged to fall on his knees with 'abject humility' to excuse 'the silence of the House at the sight of so noble a personage' when he sought to resist Wolsey's demands and, 'with many probable arguments he endeavoured to show the Cardinal that his manner of coming was neither expedient nor agreeable to the ancient liberties of the House.' But More was made of sterner stuff than one of the most odious men ever to hold the Chair, the evil Richard Rich whose perjured evidence was a fatal factor at More's trial. In the very year after More's execution, Rich cringingly referred to Henry as comparable to Solomon, 'for justice and prudence,' to Samson 'for strength and fortitude' and to Absalom 'for beauty and comeliness'.

Being Speaker during the reign of Queen Elizabeth was not the easiest of tasks, and Christopher Yelverton made the first of what became the traditional self-deprecating speech when he was elected. 'Neither from my person nor nature doth this place arise, for he that supplieth this place ought to be a man big and comely, stately and well-spoken, his voice great, his courage majestical, his nature haughty, and his purse plentiful and heavy: but the stature of my body is small, myself not so well-spoken, my voice low, my carriage lawyer-like and of the common fashion, my nature soft and bashful, my purse thin, light and never yet plentiful.'

In the seventeenth century, the Speaker, until then very much a Royal nominee, became a more genuinely independent figure, and one of the turning points in the history of the office is marked by Speaker Lenthall's rejoinder to Charles I when he came to arrest the five Members (see Chapter Two).

The next significant stage in the evolution of the Speakership came

Beautiful vaulting in the Cloisters.

in the eighteenth century with the election of Speaker Onslow. Hitherto, however independently he may have sought to assert the Commons' rights, the Speaker had never pretended to impartiality. Indeed one Speaker, Sir John Trevor, was actually expelled from the House of Commons in 1695 after he had been found guilty of accepting a bribe of 1,000 guineas from the City in order to assist the passage of a Bill. Speakers came, sometimes after contested elections, from the ruling faction or 'Party' of the day, and as the Party system evolved it became accepted that the Speaker should be of that Party rather than a nominee of the King. He was expected to use his influence for the good of his Party once he was in the Chair and not infrequently he was given Party rewards for success. Robert Harley, for instance, was Speaker for four years from 1701 before going on to become a Secretary of State and later Chancellor of the Exchequer and ultimately Lord Treasurer, and thus Prime Minister in all but name. A number of his successors earned high promotion when they vacated the Chair and there are several instances of Speakers holding Ministerial office simultaneously with their Speakership.

Daniel O'Connell, the great Irish national leader of the early nineteenth century.

With the election of Onslow in 1728, however, things changed. He remained in the Chair for thirty years and during that time established a reputation for dignity and impartiality which marks him as one of the greatest of all Speakers, and certainly the most significant constitutionally. To underline his determination to be impartial in his conduct he resigned his post as Treasurer of the Navy in 1742 and in this set an important precedent. When he retired he was awarded a pension of £3,000 and was presented with the thanks of the House 'for his constant and unwearied attendance in the Chair during the course of above thirty years in five successive Parliaments; for the unshaken integrity and impartiality of his conduct there: and for the indefatigable pains he has, with uncommon abilities, constantly taken to promote the real interest of his King and country, to maintain the honour and dignity of Parliament, and to preserve inviolable the rights and privileges of the Commons of Great Britain.' Henceforth no Speaker held ministerial office and in 1790 an Act of Parliament finally placed the Speaker above the political battlefield by granting him an annual salary of £6,000 per year, while disabling him from holding any office of profit under the Crown. Onslow's immediate successors did not, however, follow him in his example of impartiality, ('I loved independency, and pursued it.') Speaker Abbot, for instance, gave the casting vote which determined that Melville should be impeached in 1805 and made no secret of his violent opposition to any form of Catholic emancipation, and Speaker Addington briefly succeeded Pitt as Prime Minister in 1801.

But by the time of the Reform Bill impartiality had become the order of the day and after 1835 when the Whig majority refused to re-elect Sir Charles Manners-Sutton (Speaker since 1817) there was no serious attempt to prevent the re-election of any Speaker, though in 1839 and again in 1895 both major parties fielded candidates and there were closely contested elections for new Speakers.

The Victorians produced a number of eminent Speakers, the most outstanding of whom were Charles Shaw-Lefevre and Arthur Wellesley Peel, youngest son of Sir Robert Peel. It was Peel who delivered the classic definition of the office. 'I know how necessary it is for any man who aspires to fill that great office to lay aside all that is personal, all that is of Party, all that savours of political predilection, and to subordinate everything to the great interests of the House at large, to maintain not only the written law, but that unwritten law that should appeal to, as it always does appeal to, the minds and consciousness of the gentlemen of the House of Commons.' Peel, perhaps more than any other Speaker, was capable of quelling incipient riots by a mere glance. It was an invaluable attribute in a boisterous age and one not entirely shared by Speaker Gulley who once summoned the police to deal with the Irish. As a result whenever trouble was brewing in the future, some wag would shout, 'Send for the police'.

It has been well said that a good Speaker has got to know when to be deaf and when to be blind, but at the same time the House has got to know that there is a limit to his tolerance.

To keep order in a House strained by deep and conflicting passions is no easy task and to do so with a sureness and a lightness of touch is a gift given to few men. The House tries to select those who have it and once a man takes the Chair he is invested with awe-inspiring authority. He can suspend the sitting, as has happened a number of times in recent years. He can 'name' a Member (a course which inevitably leads to his suspension) if he challenges the Chair's authority. He must interpret the rules of the House and can indeed lay down new ones by establishing precedents with his judgements. And he is the one who decides who shall speak in debate, or who should ask supplementary questions of Ministers.

In addition he has a whole range of other duties and responsibilities. It is the Speaker who, at the request of the Party who held the seat, issues the Writ for a by-election. It is he who speaks for the Commons on all ceremonial occasions, as when Loyal Addresses are presented to the Sovereign, and it is he who is in charge of all the arrangements for reporting debates in the House.

On the election of a new Parliament the first thing that the assembled Members must do is elect their Speaker, and when his election has been approved (today a mere formality) by the Crown, his first task is to lay the traditional claim to the rights and privileges of the Commons, saying to the assembled Members on his return from the Lords, 'I have to report to the House that in the House of Peers . . . I have in your name, and on your behalf, laid claim by humble petition to Her Majesty, to all your ancient rights and privileges, particularly freedom of speech in debate, freedom from arrest, freedom of access to Her Majesty whenever occasion may require, and that the most favourable construction be placed on all your proceedings. All these

Keir Hardie, the first Chairman of the Parliamentary Labour Party.

163

Her Majesty has been pleased to allow and confirm, in as ample a manner as they have ever been granted or confirmed by herself or any of her royal predecessors.' The words are those that have been used for over four centuries, and each century has invested them with a new and deeper meaning and importance. Though there is much that is traditional and ceremonial about the Speaker's office (he has powers that are unlikely ever to be used again—such as the power to have an offender incarcerated for the duration of a session in the cells at the bottom of the Clock Tower) no one who knows anything of Parliament and its workings would deny that his is the most important working role within it. In a very real sense Mr Speaker is the cornerstone of our Parliamentary democracy, as well as the most distinguished inhabitant of the Palace of Westminster.

It is therefore highly appropriate that the famous lantern in Barry's best loved and best known structure which shines when the House is at work should be close to the home of the Member whose labours can never cease so long as the Parliament he serves is in being.

The light shines in the top of the Clock Tower to signify that the House is sitting at night.

CHAPTER SEVEN

A Continuing Purpose

Mr Edward Heath, Leader of the Conservative Party 1965–75 and Prime Minister 1970–74.

THE light on the Clock Tower shone brightly. Many in the unusually crowded Parliament Square on that cold winter's night were glancing towards it. They were waiting for news from within. There, the Chamber of the Commons was crammed with expectant Members who had emerged from the Division Lobbies. The benches were full. Members were sitting in the gangways and clustered around Mr Speaker's Chair at the Bar of the House. The Tellers had to push their way through the throng towards the table.

The Prime Minister in closing the debate had made it plain that he and his Government would go if they did not carry the day. Members of his Party who had doubts about the wisdom of his course, or who were flatly opposed to it, had faced a cruel dilemma. They knew that the Opposition Party, though by no means united on the issue, had agreed to vote as one. For many days, friends and colleagues had sought to persuade them that the interests of the country would best be served by the survival of the Government rather than by its replacement by a Party to which, on every other policy, they were opposed. It was unthinkable, they urged, to go into a General Election fundamentally divided on the greatest issue of the decade.

Now, as Members saw the Tellers go to the table to report the figures everyone wondered which interpretation of duty had prevailed. Few Members could remember a tenser scene, or more unhappy faces on both sides of the House. For it was obvious that many had voted, however understandable their reasons, at their Party's call rather than in conformity with long-held beliefs.

The Tellers took the place in front of the table amid a deafening roar. Many faces on the Opposition betrayed signs of heartfelt relief, not a few on the Government side of the House looked profoundly sad. The Bill was carried—by eight votes.

The Prime Minister was mobbed in the Lobby by colleagues and admiring friends who had rushed down from the Strangers' Galleries. In the Central Lobby a cry went up and the news quickly passed to those who were crowded expectantly around St Stephen's Entrance and in Parliament Square beyond.

Those with a sense of history might have recalled Macaulay's description of the passage of the Reform Bill in the Old Palace; or Disraeli's account of the splitting of the Tory Party when Peel carried the Repeal of the Corn Laws in the temporary Chamber in 1846, or

the scenes of high excitement in Barry's Chamber when Gladstone's first Home Rule Bill was defeated in 1886, and his second carried seven years later. But all those Chambers had gone and the characters who had dominated them were gone too. The date was 17 February, 1972. The House of Commons had just given a Second Reading to the Bill which was to take Britain into the Common Market. Whether the hopes of those who had voted in the 'Aye' Lobby would be realized, or the fears of those who had voted in the 'No' Lobby confirmed, there was no one at Westminster that night who doubted that an historic decision had been taken: that Parliament was very much arbiter of the nation's destiny.*

It is a role that Parliament alone can, and must, continue to fill if the Westminster system of democracy is to be preserved into the twenty-first century, if the continuing purpose of Barry's great Palace is to remain.

A study of any great institution, especially if it is intimately connected with, and embodied in, a great noble building, helps give a sense of perspective and a feeling of security and stability when times are hard and things look grim. No one who contemplates the long sweep of our national history in which events at Westminster have so often played a crucial role, and who visits the Palace conscious of that history, can fail to be reassured and to see it as a symbol of hope: the light on the Clock Tower as a beacon.

It is a common failing, and one from which politicians are by no means exempt, to emulate, however unconsciously, W. S. Gilbert's

Idiot who praises in enthusiastic tone,
Every century but this and every country but his own.

In the hundred and forty years which separated the passing of the Reform Bill and that vote on the Common Market in 1972, Westminster witnessed constant change and development, by no means confined to the destruction of the Old Palace and the painful birth of the new. As in the previous centuries of often troubled progress, new procedures evolved, new customs and habits became the order of the day. And, as always, men looked back to a mythical 'golden age' of Parliament.

At the beginning of the Victorian era there was much lamenting that, 'No Chatham, Pitt or Canning' was in the Chamber, 'to electrify a listening world by his oratory or to dazzle an admiring country by his statesmanship.' When the Queen died sixty years later, full of years and of honour, having weathered her own storms of parliamentary disapproval and unpopularity, men looked back to a new and more recent golden age in which the names of Peel and Palmerston, and, more especially, of Gladstone and Disraeli, stood out. Not that theirs were the only names to be conjured with at the turn of the century.

During the long Victorian era the old Court of Requests and Barry's

Continuing ceremony: the Conservative Government of 1970 listens to Black Rod's summons at the State Opening of Parliament.

*And in March, 1979, the Government of the day was defeated by a majority of one amid similar scenes of tension and excitement.

new Chamber had seen many statesmen and orators who had indeed, 'electrified and dazzled' their contemporaries, even if their names are now only known to Parliamentary historians. There was Stanley, (later Lord Derby) the 'Rupert of debate'. There was John Arthur Roebuck, Member for Sheffield for over twenty years, whose splendid declamatory style earned him the nickname of 'Tear'em Roebuck', an influential backbencher who never held office but whose demands for an inquiry into the conduct of the Crimean War brought down a Government. There was John Bright who, with his equally famous contemporary Richard Cobden, helped change the course of history when he persuaded Peel to embrace the cause of Tariff Reform. Bright was one of the greatest of all Parliamentary speakers. When he attacked our involvement in the Crimean War, saying that it would bring untold misery to castle, mansion and cottage, as the news of deaths on the battle front flooded in, he proclaimed, 'The Angel of Death has been abroad throughout the land: you may almost hear the beating of his wings.' As he spoke, we are told, you could almost hear the beating of the hearts of his hearers, so stilled was the Chamber.

These were the days, of course, when a man would speak for hours at a stretch. Disraeli spoke for five when he presented his first Budget: and this was not a record. Now if a Minister talks for more than an hour in introducing a major Bill there are angry and restless faces among the backbenchers anxious to deliver their own ten or fifteen minute orations. Only the debates on the Queen's Speech and on the Budget traditionally spread over several days. A hundred years ago a major debate might have lasted almost indefinitely. One on the Queen's Speech went on for sixteen days, and the Second Reading of the First Home Rule Bill in 1886 took as long, Gladstone himself speaking no less than five times, having introduced it with a speech that lasted three and a half hours. Palmerston's greatest Parliamentary performance ran, 'from the dusk of a summer evening to the dawn of a summer morning,' and for the length of his speech the Chamber was full. But in those days Parliament sat for no more than six months of the year, adjourning in mid-August and re-assembling in February (sometimes there was a brief meeting just before Christmas), and then having short recesses both at Easter and at Whitsuntide. Furthermore no votes were taken after midnight, though the House might sit long beyond, and indeed on one occasion sat continuously for forty-two hours until the Speaker, establishing a precedent, put the question, to the delight of Mr Gladstone and the anger of the Irish who had been skilfully responsible for the protracted sitting.

To give a list of those who were household names during the Victorian era would be a formidable task. The speeches of Members were reported exhaustively far beyond their constituencies, and the activities of men like Sidney Herbert, the champion of Florence Nightingale, of Cranbourne and Villiers, of Low and Milner, of Goschen and Harcourt, the Chancellor who introduced Death Duties,

Continuing tradition: searching the cellars for gunpowder on the eve of the State Opening, a custom followed every year since the Gunpowder Plot in 1605.

were eagerly followed. Lord Randolph Churchill's dramatic resignation and tragic early death were not just the talk of London drawing-rooms, and as the century turned it was men like Balfour and Chamberlain who captured the attention of the nation and gave the lie to those who had prophesied that the Victorian age would not produce figures to match the giants of the past.

There were rising stars too who could command more than an ordinary share of interest. Asquith had entered the Commons in 1886, and in 1890 the son of an obscure Welsh schoolmaster, David Lloyd George, had taken his seat. These were men destined to occupy the centre of the stage well into the twentieth century and in February 1901, within a few weeks of the old Queen's passing, a twenty-six year old soldier and former war correspondent, entered the House as Member for Oldham. Winston Churchill's Parliamentary career had begun.

The nineteenth century Parliaments are not merely memorable for their great characters and moments of high drama. Parliament as an institution was developing and evolving throughout those years. Upstairs Barry's suite of Committee Rooms was put to increasing use as the Committee system expanded and developed, and more issues were subject to detailed scrutiny.

But not all was smooth change and transition. Parliamentarians

have ever been among the most conservative of individuals. Rightly conscious of their prerogatives and privileges, they have sometimes made themselves seem foolish by the obstinate tenacity with which they have fought to resist the tides of time. Thus O'Connell, in the late 'twenties, had difficulty in taking his seat because of his Roman Catholic faith and the rigid interpretations, even when Catholic emancipation was achieved, of the Oath. Later Jewish Members fared far worse. One was fined £500 for voting in Divisions because he had not sworn to uphold the Christian faith, and Lionel de Rothschild sat for eleven years below the Bar of the House, a Member in name only, before finally, in 1858, Jews were allowed to make a protestation of allegiance which did not conflict with their consciences.

The most celebrated incident in this regard concerned the atheist Charles Bradlaugh, first elected as Member for Northampton in 1880. After six years he won his demand that he should be allowed to affirm rather than take the oath, but not before he had been unseated four times after being hauled before the Bar of the House, and, on one occasion, imprisoned in the Clock Tower.

While the Commons was reluctantly coming to terms with new manners and new thinking in the world outside, the Lords still played a central role in Parliament. The great Disraeli himself spent the greater part of his premiership in the Upper House as Lord Beaconsfield and between the passing of the Reform Bill under Earl Grey and Rosebery succeeding Gladstone in 1894, ten Cabinets were presided over by Peers. The new century was ushered in under one of the greatest of noble Prime Ministers, the Marquess of Salisbury, who, when he resigned, passed on the torch to his nephew, Arthur James Balfour. But since 1902 no Peer has held the premiership and in 1911 the powers of the Lords were severely curtailed in the Parliament Act when the predominantly Conservative House, known by the Liberals as 'Mr Balfour's Poodle', was shorn of its power of veto and merely given the chance to examine and delay measures approved in the Commons Chamber.

As the power of the Lords was reduced, so in the Commons a new Party, sprung from the working classes, was emerging. The 1832 Act had not, as some of its supporters fondly imagined, seen the end of Parliamentary reform. The franchise had been progressively extended and as early as 1874 the first 'genuine working man representative', the former miner Thomas Burt, was returned as Member for Morpeth. He was soon joined by others so that in 1885 Speaker Peel could give that dinner to 'labour representatives' (the Party as we know it was not yet born) who declined to, or were unable to, wear the costume being entertained in Speaker's House generally demanded.

Parliament's ability to adapt and absorb, however, was splendidly illustrated by Burt when, shortly after he was appointed to ministerial office in 1892 he averred that there was probably 'no place in the world where social position counts for less than in the British House of Commons'. This was a sentiment that was echoed by another working

Cleaning the building. The West Front of the House of Lords newly cleaned.

class representative, Henry Broadhurst who, as a stone-mason, had actually worked on the construction of Barry's Palace: 'In the House of Commons it mattered not what had been a man's position, nor what was the sphere of life in which he moved; if he had anything to say worth listening to he was equal to the noblest and the richest in the assembly.'

Although there was elation (and brass band-led processions) when Keir Hardie took his seat in 1892, and as the Labour Party gradually emerged as a parliamentary force, there were few real or continuing tensions within the Palace. Indeed, considering the strong conflicting passions often expressed in the Chamber, violent scenes have been extremely rare. When they have occurred, as they did briefly after

that vote on the Common Market when a Labour Member decided, in the heat of the moment, to pummel the Leader of the Liberal Party, they have almost invariably been followed by gracious apology willingly accepted. And the tension hardly ever spills over from the Chamber into the lobbies or corridors around.

No one could pretend that Parliament has found it easy to cope with the twentieth century. So often in the past the national destiny could easily be controlled from Westminster: so often this century national events have been moulded or influenced by international circumstances. But we have survived two World Wars and the leadership given in Parliament has been the crucial factor on both occasions. An Empire has been peacefully surrendered and steps, however faltering, taken to assume a new European role and to grapple with new frustrations and new aspirations within the United Kingdom. The commonest cry both within the Chamber and without in recent years has been a variation of the 'where are the giants of old?' theme. How often are Members of Parliament assailed by their constituents with the question, 'When will there be another Churchill?'

Chathams and Churchills and Disraelis do not occur in every Parliamentary generation but the post-war parliaments have not been without their significant figures. Clement Attlee was one and Harold Macmillan another, and Edward Heath was strangely reminiscent of Peel in that he held his position by strength of character rather than by bonds of affection, and, like Peel, set his country on a new course in the process. It may not be as true as when Chesterfield wrote to his son in 1749 that 'You must first make a figure there [in Parliament] if you would make a figure in the country.' The power of the Trade Union barons, and of the press and the captains of industry may be significantly exercised outside Westminster but the fact is that still some of the brightest and the best seek to make their mark in the House of Commons. Whenever a constituency falls vacant there are hundreds of applicants anxious to display their talents to the occupying party's Selection Committee.

This is not to deny that there has been a decline in public respect for Parliament, though anybody who feels inclined to look at eighteenth century cartoons, or at some of the more vitriolic outpourings of Victorian times, should feel somewhat reassured.

Parliament, however, needs to stand higher in public esteem and Members could profitably ponder Disraeli's observation about 'that public opinion whose mild and irresistible influence can control even the decrees of Parliament and without whose support the most august and ancient institutions are but "the baseless fabric of a vision".' There is still a place for vision, and perhaps the regular broadcasting of parliamentary proceedings will help to make more people aware of what goes on in the Palace of Westminster and appreciate that there, for all its imperfections, is the best guardian of their liberties. Then they might see Barry's great Palace for what it truly is: a People's Palace in which the freedom of the individual can be far better

Mrs Margaret Thatcher, the first woman Prime Minister of Great Britain.

172

The latest addition — the fountain erected by Parliament in New Palace Yard to mark the Jubilee of Queen Elizabeth II in 1977.

guarded, and his aspirations far more nobly challenged, than in any of those falsely named 'peoples' palaces' in régimes where democracy has been extinguished, or never given a chance to flourish.

In the prayer that is used in both Houses of Parliament at the beginning of every day's sitting Members ask that, 'laying aside all private interests, prejudices and partial affections, the result of all our counsels may be to the glory of Thy blessed Name, the maintenance of true Religion and Justice, the safety, honour and happiness of the Queen, the public wealth, peace and tranquillity of the Realm, and the uniting and knitting together of the hearts of all persons and estates within the same, in true Christian love and Charity, one towards another.'

Not many Members attend prayers. Many are not Christians. In their practices and beliefs they mirror fairly accurately those of their constituents, so many of whom are agnostic, atheist, or of other faiths.

There can, however, be very few at Westminster, or in the country, who would not endorse the sentiments of the prayer. Successive generations of Members have sought, often very imperfectly, to endorse them in the service that they have rendered. There is little reason to doubt that future generations will do likewise and that Barry's great Palace of Westminster will continue to provide inspiration to those who work within and recollect their past, and to those who send them there.

Many who go will not achieve greatness, nor have it thrust upon them, but in the collective confidence of the electorate in the collective wisdom of their representatives lies our hope, a hope to which a great architect gave a noble focus in a building which it is our common privilege to enjoy and our common duty to preserve.

CHRONOLOGY

A few key dates in the history of the Palace: this brief chronology aims to help the reader to set some of the main events described in this book in a wider context.

	WESTMINSTER	GENERAL
1065	Edward the Confessor's Westminster Abbey consecrated	
1066		The Norman Conquest
1097	William II orders building of Westminster Hall	
1102	Henry I summons his first great council at Westminster	
1215		Sealing of Magna Carta
1265	First Parliament to include representatives from shires and boroughs summoned to Westminster by Simon de Montfort.	
1272		Accession of Edward I
1295	Model Parliament meets	
1305	Trial of William Wallace in Westminster Hall	
1314		Battle of Bannockburn
1348–9		The Black Death
1381		The Peasants' Revolt
1394–9	Rebuilding of Westminster Hall by Richard II—architect Henry Yevele	
1415		Battle of Agincourt
1431		Death of Joan of Arc
1485		Battle of Bosworth
1509	Accession of Henry VIII (Last king to live in the Palace)	
1520		Field of Cloth of Gold
1533		Excommunication of Henry VIII—break with Rome complete
1535	Trials of Sir Thomas More and Bishop John Fisher	
1547	Edward VI gives the Chapel of St Stephen to the Commons as their Chamber	
1549		First English Prayer Book
1558		Accession of Queen Elizabeth I
1587		Execution of Mary, Queen of Scots
1588		Defeat of the Spanish Armada
1603		Accession of James I
1605	The Gundpowder Plot	
1606	Trial and execution of the Conspirators	
1618–48		The Thirty Years' War

	WESTMINSTER	GENERAL
1625	Accession of Charles I	
1626	Buckingham impeached	
1628	The Petition of Right	
1637	Trial of Hampden	
1640	The Short Parliament	
	The Long Parliament meets (*Nov.*)	
1641	Execution of Strafford	
1642	Attempt to arrest the Five Members (*Jan.*)	Start of the Civil War (*Aug.*) Battle of Edgehill (*Oct.*)
1645		Battle of Naseby
1648	Pride's Purge	
1649	Trial of Charles I in Westminster Hall	
	Cromwell proclaimed Lord Protector in	
1653	Westminster Hall—expulsion of the Rump Parliament.	
	Restoration of Charles II—meeting of	
1660	Restoration Parliament	
1661–79	Cavalier Parliament	
1665		The Great Plague
1666		The Fire of London
1678		The Popish Plot
1679	New Parliament meets	
1685		Accession of James II
1688	Trial of the Seven Bishops	
		Flight of James II: Accession of William and Mary
1689	Bill of Rights	
1690		Battle of the Boyne
1704		Battle of Blenheim
1707	Act of Union between England and Scotland	
1714		Accession of George I (first Hanoverian King)
1715	Trial of leaders of first Jacobite Rebellion	First Jacobite Rebellion (the Fifteen)
1721–42	Ministry of Sir Robert Walpole	
1745		Second Jacobite Rebellion (The Forty-Five)
1746	Trial of leaders of second Jacobite Rebellion	
1756–63		The Seven Years' War
1757–61	Ministry of William Pitt the Elder	
1764	First expulsion of John Wilkes from House of Commons	
1775–83		The American War of Independence
1783	Pitt the Younger becomes Prime Minister	
1788–95	Trial of Warren Hastings	
1789		Start of the French Revolution
1805		Battle of Trafalgar
1812	Assassination of Spencer Perceval in the Members' Lobby	
1815		Battle of Waterloo

	WESTMINSTER	GENERAL
1822	Trial of Queen Caroline the House of Lords	
1832	Reform Bill passed	
1834	Destruction of Old Palace of Westminster by fire	
1837	Accession of Queen Victoria	
1840	Foundation stone of New Palace laid by Mrs Barry	
1846	Repeal of the Corn Laws	
1847	House of Lords occupies new Chamber	
1850	House of Commons occupies new Chamber	
1852	Death of Pugin	
1853–6		Crimean War
1857		Indian Mutiny
1859	Big Ben goes into service	
1860	Death of Charles Barry	
1886	Bradlaugh admitted to Parliament	
1899–1902		Boer War
1901		Death of Queen Victoria: Accession of Edward VII
1914–18		First World War
1916	Lloyd George becomes Prime Minister	
1919	Lady Astor, first woman M.P. takes her seat	
1922		Irish Free State established
1924	First Labour Government	
1926		The General Strike
1931	Statute of Westminster	
1936		The Abdication Crisis: Accession of King George VI
1939–45		Second World War
1940	Churchill becomes Prime Minister	
1941	Destruction of Chamber of House of Commons by enemy action	
1950	Opening of rebuilt Chamber: architect Sir Gilbert Scott	
1952	Death of King George VI: Accession of Queen Elizabeth II	
1956		The Suez Crisis
1957		The Treaty of Rome (E.E.C.)
1965	Lying in state of Sir Winston Churchill in Westminster Hall Seventh Centenary celebrations of de Montfort's parliament	
1972	Parliament votes for entry to E.E.C.	
1977	Presentation of loyal Address to Elizabeth II in Westminster Hall on her Jubilee	
1979	Assassination of Airey Neave in New Palace Yard	
1979	First woman Prime Minister, Margaret Thatcher, addresses the House	

FOR FURTHER READING

I have had many fascinating hours browsing through old journals, Committee reports, newspapers, and other contemporary records, particularly those describing the fire of 1834 and the building of the New Palace. I have drawn on many of these but felt it wrong to fill the book with footnotes as I have also consulted a multitude of published works, many alas now out of print. The ones I have listed here are merely some of those which I think the interested reader would find particularly enjoyable and which should, whether in print or not, be available from most good libraries.

THE OLD PALACE
Brayley, E. W. and Britton, John: *History of the Ancient Palace of Westminster* (London, 1836)
Smith, J. T.: *Antiquities of Westminster* (London, 1807)

HISTORY AND WORKING OF PARLIAMENT
Ilbert, Sir Courtney: *Parliament, its History, Constitution, and Practice* (O.U.P., 1911) revised by Sir Cecil Carr and published in Home University Library Series, 1948)
Jennings, Sir Ivor: *Parliament* (Cambridge, 1939)
Mackenzie, Kenneth: *The English Parliament* (Penguin, 1950)
Rhodes, James Robert: *An Introduction to the House of Commons* (Collins, 1961)
Saunders, Hilary St George: *Westminster Hall* (Michael Joseph, 1951)
Taylor, Eric S.: *The House of Commons at Work* (Penguin, 1951)
Wright, Arnold and Smith P.: *Parliament Past and Present* (London 1902)

THE BUILDING
Pope Hennessey, John: *The Palace of Westminster* (Michael Joseph, 1974)—an excellent but very brief monograph.
Port, Michael Harry: (edited) *The Houses of Parliament* (Yale, 1976)—the most exhaustive book on the architecture and art of the Palace of Westminster.
Stanton, Phoebe: *Pugin* (Thames and Hudson, 1971)
Mordaunt Crook, J. and Port, M. H.: *The History of the King's Works* (H.M.S.O., 1973)
Clark, Lord: *The Gothic Revival* (John Murray, 1962)
Cocks, Barnet: *Mid-Victorian Masterpiece* (Hutchinson, 1977) for which I am grateful for the quotation on p. 157.

HISTORY, MEMOIRS AND BIOGRAPHIES
Here the task of selection is virtually impossible and hideously invidious. Any reader unacquainted with particular aspects of English history of any period can do no better than consult the appropriate volume in *The Oxford History of England* and be guided by its bibliography. Those fascinated by biographies will be glad to know that the monumental *Dictionary of National Biography* (Oxford University Press) is now available in an inexpensive two volume edition, complete with magnifying glass. One of the most fascinating of all series to browse through is R. Cobbet's *Complete Collection of State Trials* published in ten volumes between 1809 and 1811.

Below I have listed a very few works of special interest:

Blake, Robert: *Disraeli* (Eyre and Spottiswoode, 1966)
Grant, James: *Random Recollections of the House of Commons* (London, 1836)
Harvey, John H.: *Henry Yevele, c. 1300–1400 The Life of An English Architect* (B. T. Batsford, 1944)
Hemingford, Lord: *Back-Bencher and Chairman* (John Murray, 1946)
Herbert, Alan: *Independent Member* (Methuen, 1950)
Lucy, Sir Henry: *Peeps at Parliament* (George Newnes, 1903)
Lucy, Sir Henry: *Later Peeps at Parliament* (George Newnes, 1905)
Magnus, Sir Philip: *Gladstone* (John Murray, 1954)
Neil, J. E.: *The Elizabethan House of Commons* (Cape, 1949)
Passingham: *A History of the Coronation* (London, 1936)
Wedgewood, C. V.: *The Trial of Charles I* (Collins, 1964)
Winterton, Rt. Hon Earl: *Orders of the Day* (Cassell, 1953)

MISCELLANEOUS
King, Horace Maybray: *Before Hansard* (J. M. Dent, 1968)
Marsden, Philip: *The Officers of the Commons* (H.M.S.O., 1979)
Selwyn-Lloyd, Lord: *Mr Speaker, Sir* (Jonathan Cape, 1976)

179